RESIDENTIAL MODERNISM REBORN
CALIFORNIA COOL

RESIDENTIAL MODERNISM REBORN
CALIFORNIA COOL

TEXT AND PHOTOGRAPHY BY
RUSSELL ABRAHAM
ASMP

images Publishing

Published in Australia in 2010 by
The Images Publishing Group Pty Ltd
ABN 89 059 734 431
6 Bastow Place, Mulgrave, Victoria 3170, Australia
Tel: +61 3 9561 5544 Fax: +61 3 9561 4860
books@imagespublishing.com
www.imagespublishing.com

Copyright © The Images Publishing Group Pty Ltd 2010
The Images Publishing Group Reference Number:

All rights reserved. Apart from any fair dealing for the purposes of private study, research, criticism or review as permitted under the Copyright Act, no part of this publication may be reproduced, stored in a retrieval system or transmitted in any form by any means, electronic, mechanical, photocopying, recording or otherwise, without the written permission of the publisher.

National Library of Australia Cataloguing-in-Publication entry:

Author:	Abraham, Russell.
Title:	California cool : residential modernism reborn / Russell Abraham.
ISBN:	9781864703986 (hbk.)
Subjects:	Architecture, Modern—21st century—California
	Architecture, Modern—20th century—California
	Architecture, Domestic—California
	Architecture and climate—California
	Architecture—American influences
Dewey Number:	720.9794

Edited by Beth Browne

Production by The Graphic Image Studio Pty Ltd, Mulgrave, Australia
www.tgis.com.au

Pre-publishing services by United Graphic Pte Ltd, Singapore
Printed on 150 gsm Quatro Silk Matt paper by Everbest Printing Co. Ltd., in Hong Kong/China

IMAGES has included on its website a page for special notices in relation to this and its other publications. Please visit www.imagespublishing.com.

Contents

6 Introduction: How Modernism Found a Home in California
Russell Abraham

Hillside Houses

12 Stroke of Genius in the Palisades
Cigolle X Coleman

28 A Modernist Look at Bay Area Regionalism
WA design

44 A Bay View That Can't Be Beat
Kanner Architects

58 Hollywood Hills House: Life in the Fast Lane
Studio Pali Fekete architects [SPF:a]

68 Hillside Houses North of San Francisco
Swatt Architects

84 Modernism: Elegant and Reproducible
Ray Kappe, FAIA

Urban Living

94 A House of Steel for a Man of Glass in West Berkeley
Regan Bice Architects

102 Big City Architect, Big City House
Johnson Fain

112 Modernism, San Francisco Style
Craig Steely Architecture

120 A Line from Craig Ellwood to the Present
Macy Architecture

130 Two Venetian Cousins
Callas Shortridge architects

Beach Houses

146 The House is a (Recycled) Machine for Living
David Hertz Architects Inc., Studio of Environmental Architecture

158 Beach Town Houses, North and South
Ehrlich Architects

172 Life on the Water
Seidel Architects

178 Beachside Fun
Studio 9 one 2

186 Working with a "Postage Stamp" Lot
Dean Nota Architect

194 Upbeat Modern in a Quirky Monterey Bay Town
Flesher + Foster Architects

Country Houses

208 A Master's Touch in Carmel Valley
Jerrold E Lomax, FAIA: Architect

218 Getting Down to Basics
Jim Jennings Architecture

226 Desert Living, Prefabricated
Marmol Radziner

238 Wine Country Simplicity
Edmonds + Lee

250 Acknowledgments

251 Index of Architects

How Modernism Found a Home in California

Russell Abraham

The average temperature in Dessau, Germany, the original home of the Bauhaus School of Design, is a chilly −2 °C in January. In Los Angeles, California, it's just north of 22 °C. It rains close to 1.5 meters each year in central Germany. In Los Angeles, annual rainfall is around 24 centimeters. If the key function of architecture is to shelter its inhabitants from the elements, one has to wonder what Walter Gropius, the seminal modernist architect and founder of the Bauhaus, thought at his atelier in Dessau in the early 1920s when he and Ludwig Mies van der Rohe created a style of architecture called the International style, more commonly known in the United States as modernism. This style was a radical departure from the historicism and eclecticism of architecture in the 19th century. Using newly available building materials, like plate glass, reinforced concrete, and structural steel, these radical architects fashioned an architecture that became the paradigm for building in the second half of the 20th century in most of the industrialized world.

Modernism stripped buildings of most ornamentation. It opened up interior space and significantly blurred the line between outside and inside. Thin, horizontal, cantilevered planes replaced gabled roofs. Ribbons of steel replaced brick columns. Well-ordered fenestration gave way to walls of glass. Walls disappeared, roofs disappeared, and columns disappeared. Buildings essentially became cellophane envelopes. In short, the International style was the architecture most appropriate for a climate where the outside temperatures hovers around a balmy 25 °C year-round, and the annual rainfall can be measured in centimeters rather than meters. The International style was a poor architectural solution for cold and wet central Europe.

Unbeknown to Gropius and Mies in the 1920s, the perfect environment for their new architecture was a mere 10,000 kilometers to the west.

California has always been a cultural enigma. It has been both the cutting edge and the rear guard of many cultural phenomena in the United States and the Western world. Its rapidly changing, vastly heterogeneous society has seen the best and the worst of America's social, political, and artistic history. The film and entertainment industry in the south and the technology industry in the north have created thousands of overnight millionaires, many creating cultural change with their lifestyles. What is responsible for this phenomenon? Adolf Hitler's cultural paranoia and ethnic bigotry in the 1930s resulted in many of Germany's most creative people fleeing Nazi oppression to find a welcoming home in the great metropolises of Los Angeles and San Francisco. This migration included hundreds of German and Austrian film actors, cinematographers, and modernist architects.

The likes of Richard Neutra and Rudolph Schindler found in Los Angeles an open hand and an open mind to their new ideas about architecture. Consequently, starting in the late 1920s and early 1930s, these architectural pioneers sowed the seeds of modernism on the West Coast. Since coastal California's climate affords the opportunity to live outside comfortably year-round, the architecture of the Bauhaus was culturally and environmentally a perfect fit. In Los Angeles, for example, roses bloom in January, lilies in February, and jacarandas in March. Gracious palm trees line the boulevards. Because it rarely rains, flat roofs make perfect sense. Because the ambient temperature varies so little from winter to summer, walls of

Left: Case Study House 22, Pierre Koenig, architect; photo printed with permission from Stahl House, Inc.

glass also make perfect sense. And finally, because much of coastal California lies in a range of low-slung mountains and rolling hills, houses perched on hillsides with expansive views are similarly appropriate. California was ultimately the Shangri-La for the International style, though very few people knew it in 1925.

The Second World War left much of Europe in ashes but most of the United States physically untouched. Despite this fact, very little new building other than large public works projects happened in the United States during the 1930s. The Great Depression had collapsed the country's economic system, while almost half the banks in the United States disappeared between 1929 and 1936. Thus, while ideas for a new social order and a new architecture percolated among artists, architects, and intellectuals, the finances for building that new world were nevertheless a decade away.

Beginning in the early 1940s, the US economy quickly became heavily based on consumerism. During the war, California was the staging area for much of the Pacific theater. The U.S. government sent millions of G.I.s to California military bases to work in supply depots, or off to battle overseas, but when the war ended many either stayed in or returned to California for its favorable climate. A great explosion of suburban sprawl, fueled by new highways and affordable private automobiles, resulted. The greenbelts of small family "truck farms" surrounding many American cities became the fertile fields of the new suburbs. And between 1940 and 1960, California's population more than doubled from 6.9 million to 15.7 million. This all amounted to a massive building boom, requiring, in turn, a style.

Modernism provided this style as it went from academia to Main Street. Walter Gropius and Mies van der Rohe had left Germany and found their way to Harvard and the University of Illinois. Their students were the vanguard of the modernist movement in the United States. It first popped up in high-rises and commercial buildings in New York, Chicago, and Los Angeles. But could modernism make the jump to the residential side of architecture? One man thought it could, and he tested his ideas in Los Angeles. John Entenza was the editor of Arts & Architecture magazine and a strong advocate for modernism. He believed the style should be the new paradigm for residential architecture, and to promote that ideal he began a program to commission modernist architects in Los Angeles and San Francisco to design and build contemporary modernist houses that would serve as case studies.

In 1948, Arts & Architecture commissioned and built six modernist Case Study Houses in Los Angeles. Entenza appointed Charles Eames, Richard Neutra, Craig Ellwood, William Wurster, and Raphael Soriano to the program. The Case Study Houses, many photographed by renowned architectural photographer Julius Shulman, became symbols of residential modernism in California and around the world. In total, there were 28 houses designed and/or built over an 18-year period, but it was the early Case Study Houses built from 1948 to 1955 that established the modern style in California. These Case Study Houses became the new paradigm for modernism in the United States in much the same way that Le Courbusier's Villa Savoye did a generation earlier in Europe.

Even though the Case Study Houses were immensely popular, modern residential architecture remained the purview of the cognoscenti. Most middle-class Americans loved looking at the daring designs proffered by avant-garde architects, but preferred living in merchant-built "ranchers." Modernism remained the style of commercial architecture and the taste of the elite.

Starting in the late 1990s and continuing to this day, modernist residential architecture has experienced an unexpected revival. It continues to be rediscovered, reinterpreted, and revived as the preferred residential style among a forward-thinking and prosperous class of Californians. The modern homes of the 1950s have become collector's items along with Saarinen chairs and Noguchi tables. From high-rise condominium projects in San Francisco and San Jose to cool beach-town homes in Venice and Hermosa Beach, modernism has, once again, left its unmistakable mark on the California landscape. In the 60 years since the first Case Study Houses, materials and building technologies have changed significantly, allowing for more innovation and invention. Straight lines have given way to curves. Glass and concrete have been improved so that they are lighter, stronger, and better at reflecting heat. Today there are modern houses built using everything from recycled timber and concrete to sheet titanium or zinc. Despite such improvements, the principles set down in Dessau, Germany 80 years ago remain the same: let the natural character of the material be its aesthetic.

Gropius and Mies did not make it to California. One can only wonder what would have happened if they did. It is one of the ironies of history that the theories of great thinkers are often misplaced in time and place. And the ironies abound. Germany, essentially destroyed in the Second World War, chose to rebuild its cities using the 19th-century eclectic model. However, the United States, whose cities were perfectly intact at the end of the war, embraced the paradigm of modernism, transforming the cores of almost every one of its major cities.

This book looks both backward and forward, and includes the current work of modernism's living masters as well as its youthful practitioners. Ray Kappe and Jerrold Lomax worked in Los Angeles on Case Study Houses from the 1950s. They still practice and some of their new work is in this book. At the same time, there is a solid core of their protégés who have been creating modernist houses for the past 30 years. Architects such as Robert Swatt, Dean Nota, Steve Ehrlich, Jim Jennings, and Stephen Kanner have active practices and are producing exceptional work. Finally, the book features a third group, young architects like Craig Steely, Zoltan Pali, and David Stark Wilson, who are reinterpreting the modernist paradigm in innovative ways. Several of these architects incorporate prefabrication and sustainability in their designs. Many of the houses in this book are completely energy self-sufficient, and some even have gray-water systems to help compensate for California's semi-arid climate. Also explored are the backgrounds, personalities, and some of the design philosophies of these architects, hopefully giving the reader some insight into why their work looks the way it does.

A building certainly has to fulfill its primary functional requirements of providing shelter, utility, and security to its inhabitants. A building becomes architecture only when it begins to make a meaningful statement about the society in which it exists. In an uncanny way, the architect becomes both a creator of powerful symbols and a mirror to the society in which she or he lives. All the houses selected for this book make strong statements about the architects, their owners, and society. They are symbols of California's uninhibited, innovative, and adventurous culture. From tiny beach-town lots and congested cities to expansive country estates, each house in this book is emblematic of California's avant-garde culture. Modernism, created in the 20th century, has been reinvented in California as the new architectural paradigm for the 21st century.

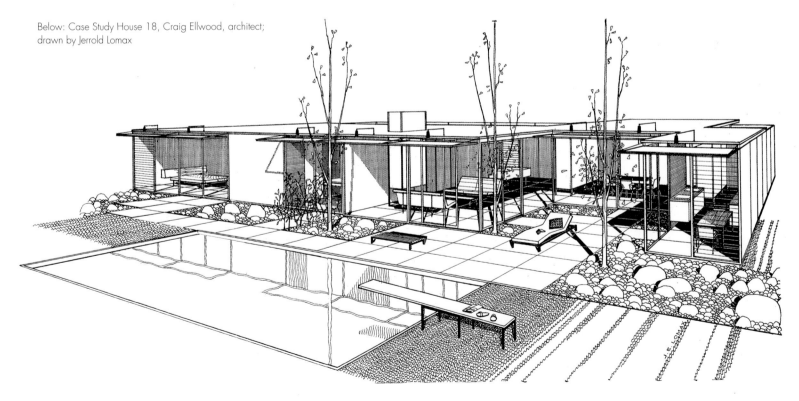

Below: Case Study House 18, Craig Ellwood, architect; drawn by Jerrold Lomax

HILLSIDE HOUSES

1

Stroke of Genius in the Palisades
Cigolle X Coleman

Mark Cigolle and Kim Coleman, a husband and wife architectural team, divide their time between professional practice and design teaching. While their portfolio is not large, each of their buildings is an architectural tour de force that turns heads and demands recognition. Their work is crisp, innovative, and breathtaking. Finding new uses for traditional materials and using new materials for architectural expression, the architecture of Cigolle X Coleman continually pushes the envelope of modernism.

Mark Cigolle, a graduate of Princeton University, began his architectural career in the office of Michael Graves, the celebrated postmodernist, and moved on to work with some of the most talented architects in New York in the 1970s, including Richard Meier and Peter Eisenman. After teaching at The University of Kentucky and Rhode Island School of Design, Cigolle took a visiting professorship at the University of Virginia, where he met his wife and partner Kim Coleman. Coleman had worked in Washington D.C. doing historic restoration and general contracting and was earning a master's degree in architecture at UVA. Mark, almost on a whim, came to Los Angeles in the early 1980s and accepted a teaching position at the University of Southern California. After a first year of discovery, they found opportunities to adapt their lives and work to the Southern California aesthetic, seeing each of their projects as a chance to experiment with different programmatic, site, and material ideas.

A portion of the practice focuses on the design of houses for Kim, Mark, and their family to live in. They design the house, oversee the construction and, over the course of a few years, they fine-tune the work, sell it, and then start another project. Today, Kim teaches full-time at the University of Southern California, where she is the chair of undergraduate architecture, while Mark oversees the studio. They both have an active hand in the design process. Kim spoke about their current house, saying that, like all the houses they create for themselves, this one is a laboratory for experimentation that will only be completed when they have left it.

The TR-2 house sits on a slope a few hundred meters from the Pacific at the most northwesterly edge of Los Angeles. From the street the house appears to be two zinc-and-glass boxes, one of smooth, flat panels and the other wrapped in perforated corrugated sheets, set at 90 degrees to one another, but the plan is more intricate. The main house is actually three volumes, two visible and one hidden. The piano nobile is embedded into the sloping site and treated as an outdoor room, wrapped in glass on all sides and fronted by a terrace and lap pool. Suspended above is a larger volume that encloses bedrooms and private living spaces and provides a sunscreen. A lower-level concrete volume, hidden by a sod roof that becomes a green extension for the main space, serves as the guest quarters and a media/music studio for the family.

The adjacent steel-frame structure supports the studio, an elevated glass volume over an open parking platform. The studio is connected to the house by an open steel bridge with stainless steel grating.

The upper volume of the house is set on steel columns placed approximately 5 meters apart over an open-plan living space with the only enclosure being the WC, which is carefully hidden behind mirrors and a translucent cellular plastic wall. The kitchen casework sits on 20-centimetre-tall legs, adding to the illusion that it is floating. Almost all of the furniture, much of which is designed by the firm, sits on large wheels and is moveable. At the center is a grand staircase, half concrete and half folded steel plate, which leads to a second-floor gallery surrounding an atrium. Photovoltaic panels are imbedded into the atrium skylights (and also the south face of the studio) and serve both as a sunshade and power source. The master bedroom is separated from the gallery by a series of sliding glass panels with sandwiched cellular plastic sheeting that provide both light and privacy. The dramatic white curtains in the master bedroom and studio are fabricated from Swedish Army camouflage material. Throughout the house, simple materials are used in innovative ways to create a unique ambience that is totally modern. Sitting in the main space, one can roll open the 4-meter-high glass doors and take in the expanse of the Pacific Ocean's sandy beaches and the Santa Monica Mountains stretching off into the distant horizon. Open, bright, and robust, the TR-2 house is emblematic of the best of Southern California modern design.

A Modernist Look at Bay Area Regionalism
WA design

David Stark Wilson looks like he could be more at home climbing a mountain in California's Sierra Nevada than sitting behind a drafting table. In fact, that is what he does for fun. An accomplished outdoorsman, he has spent much of his personal life climbing in the Sierras and other equally challenging ranges on four continents. He is also an accomplished photographer who has produced two books of his photographic work.

Wilson was born in Berkeley and graduated with a degree in mathematics from the University of California. While still at Berkeley he started designing furniture and working on small building projects to help finance his education. After graduating from Berkeley, Wilson decided that the world of architecture held more promise than the world of mathematics. He founded the firm WA Design shortly after graduating. Wilson confesses that he "just wasn't smart enough to be one of the world's great mathematicians." Mathematics may have lost a star, but architecture in the San Francisco Bay Area certainly gained one. Surrounded by significant historical buildings in his hometown of Berkeley, he was influenced by the work of Bernard Maybeck, an early 20th-century architect who designed many of Berkeley's buildings. Maybeck's work was often subtle modernist architecture wrapped in a craftsman or neoclassical envelope. He was a proponent of the Bay Area shingle style and his residential work was similar to Frank Lloyd Wright's Oak Park period.

Wilson's work is a clever blend of mid-20th-century modern and Bay regional styles. He is not afraid to use saturated colors, pitched rooflines, or barrel-vaulted ceilings. All of his work is beautifully detailed, often using traditional materials in non-traditional ways. The Vicente house, built on a sloping lot in the Berkeley Hills, is no exception. The area was devastated by a huge wildfire in 1991, which destroyed many of the homes on this street and the adjacent neighborhoods. What remained were a handful of traditional manor homes from the 1920s and numerous scorched home sites. Wilson's task, along with his colleague Chris Parlette, was to create a distinctive, modernist building that did not clash with its few remaining traditional neighbors.

The Berkeley house comprises three separate structures built around a hardscaped courtyard with large planters and gardens. A raised lap pool runs between two of the buildings separating the public structure from the private one. Upon entry through the front door of the main building, the wood-paneled ceiling soars upward, inviting one into the open living space. Slanting walls and somber-hued plaster finishes create a womb-like environment that opens onto a bright internal courtyard. The main building connects to the secondary structure with a glass-enclosed corridor that also acts as a divider for the courtyard. The second building serves as sleeping quarters with the master bedroom and bathroom on the second floor. A deck off the master suite affords sweeping views of the bay and San Francisco beyond. At the back of the second building is a cozy sitting room.

Built on a relatively steep upslope, the courtyard between the three buildings serves as a level outdoor living space for entertaining and enjoying the Bay Area's almost year-round spring-like climate. Pitched roofs with deep eaves and large solid zinc shingles are reminiscent of Maybeck's houses a century earlier. Red steel columns support the roofs of each structure and create a distinct rhythm next to the house's earthen-hued exteriors. Viewed from either the courtyard or street, the red columns and sloping roof lines create a set of arresting façades. The Berkeley house, modernist in almost every way, pays quiet respect to the Bay Area shingle style tradition.

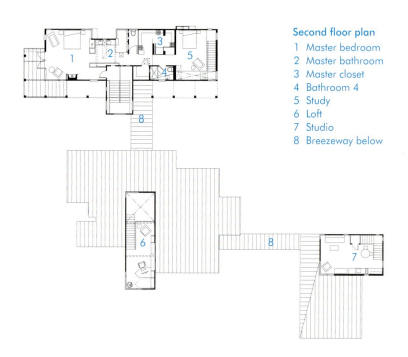

Second floor plan

1. Master bedroom
2. Master bathroom
3. Master closet
4. Bathroom 4
5. Study
6. Loft
7. Studio
8. Breezeway below

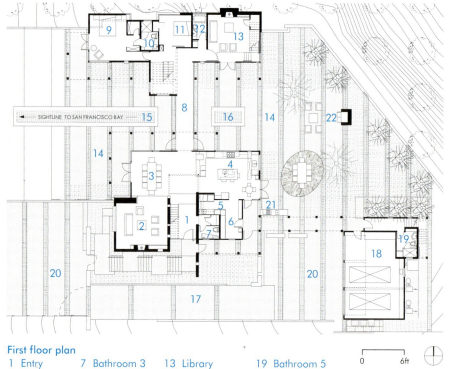

First floor plan

1. Entry
2. Living
3. Dining
4. Kitchen
5. Laundry
6. Pantry
7. Bathroom 3
8. Breezeway
9. Bedroom 1
10. Bathroom 1
11. Bedroom 2
12. Bathroom 2
13. Library
14. Patio
15. Pool
16. Heated pool
17. Driveway
18. Garage
19. Bathroom 5
20. Parking court
21. Grill area
22. Outdoor fireplace

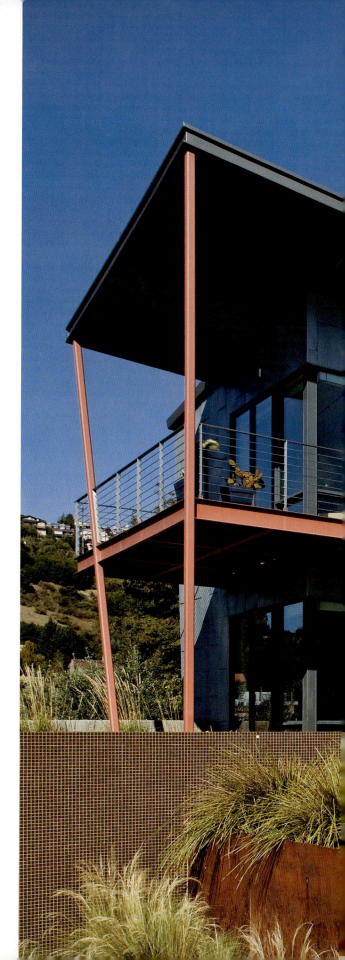

A Bay View That Can't Be Beat

Kanner Architects

The city of Los Angeles and architecture have been entwined around Stephen Kanner most of his life. He is a third-generation architect and a lifelong resident of the city. His father was a contemporary of the great cultural heroes of mid-20th-century design, many of them personal friends. As a boy he remembers Charles Eames and Buckminster Fuller stopping by for dinner. In high school and college, Kanner excelled in a variety of fine arts, but he made the choice to pursue a career in architecture after gaining his professional degree from the University of California at Berkeley.

After school, Kanner decided to see what life was like outside Southern California, so he moved to Boston and found a job with Cambridge Seven Architects, working on a variety of significant projects. He jumped at the opportunity to return to Southern California when he was offered a job at the L.A. office of Skidmore Owings & Merrill in the early 1980s. Boston's long, snowy winters had sent him home. In 1983 he joined his father, Charles, at Kanner Architects. Since that time his firm has completed a large number of projects across the building spectrum and won numerous awards, but single-family projects are still an important part of the firm's work.

Kanner sees himself as more than an architect. He is the founder of the Architecture + Design Museum in Los Angeles and a past president of the American Institute of Architects L.A. chapter. He makes a point of knowing who is doing what and acting as a patron and spokesperson for the L.A. architectural community. His openness and kindness is apparent and without reservation.

Kanner brings the same creativity to designing an outlandish In-N-Out Burger restaurant in West L.A. as he does to a high-rise on Wilshire Boulevard. That is why his firm has won more than 25 regional and national awards in the past five years. Its work is always provocative and "out of the box" architecture.

The Broadway Terrace house was built on one of the few unbuilt lots remaining from the 1991 firestorm that destroyed much of the hillside community behind the cities of Berkeley and Oakland. These hillside lots are narrow, steep, and hazardous during the fire season of late summer and early fall, but the views are breathtaking and the Bay Area climate quite mild most of the year. The house is composed of two buildings that step down the hill and are connected with an enclosed, glazed bridge. The larger main building faces the view and contains both the major public spaces and the master bedroom suite. Opening out to the west with expansive window walls and decks, all of the main spaces have sweeping views of Oakland, the bay, and San Francisco on the horizon. The form of the main structure shoots out like a giant letter L with a chamfered edge. The window wall is set back, allowing space for decks and overhangs to keep the glare of the intense California sun limited to the very late afternoon. For privacy and fire-suppression purposes, the side walls of each building are mostly windowless stucco with a gentle concave curve. In plan, they look like two inverted parentheses. The stucco has a raked finish that catches the light in a random checkered pattern that

breaks the monotony of the large white surfaces. The structural steel moment frame that gives the house its seismic strength is articulated by significant wide-flanges that rise from floor to ceiling in the corners of the room and become a design element.

The 1991 Oakland Hills fire destroyed more than 3,000 homes, though most have been rebuilt with widely varying results. Some people chose to just replicate the original cottages while others saw the need to build their own mini-mansion, albeit on a 1,000-square-meter lot. A few houses were the sensitive creations of smart, talented architects who understood the need to create appropriate, yet stimulating, buildings on difficult sites. The Broadway Terrace home can easily be counted among those few homes.

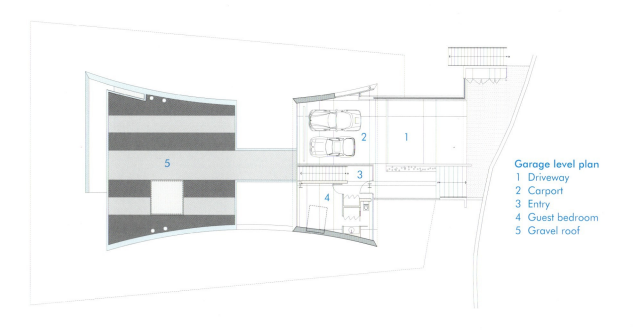

Garage level plan
1. Driveway
2. Carport
3. Entry
4. Guest bedroom
5. Gravel roof

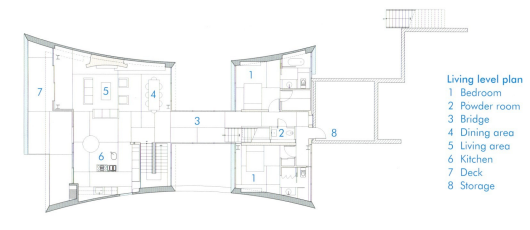

Living level plan
1. Bedroom
2. Powder room
3. Bridge
4. Dining area
5. Living area
6. Kitchen
7. Deck
8. Storage

Master level plan
1. Master bedroom
2. Master bathroom
3. Master closet
4. Laundry
5. Garden courtyard
6. Infinity pool deck

51

Hollywood Hills House: Life in the Fast Lane

Studio Pali Fekete architects [SPF:a]

Zoltan Pali is a man of contradictions. He is a foreigner and a native son. He is a professor of architecture who never earned a degree in architecture. His work is immensely creative and yet he considers himself a technician. He is both gruff and extremely kind. He lives above his studio in a newly developing part of Los Angeles with his partner Judit Fekete and two sons. He is an urban pioneer—an outsider and an insider.

Pali entered the profession through the back door. On his father's advice, he majored in engineering at the University of California, Los Angeles. A competent professional draftsman, he supported himself through college by creating working drawings for architectural firms. As it turned out, engineering was not for him and since UCLA did not have an undergraduate program in architecture he transferred to the fine arts program hoping to do graduate work in architecture. After graduation, he applied to two different architectural schools to enter their degree programs but was unsuccessful. Undeterred, he apprenticed with Jerrold Lomax, one of the leading modernist architects in Southern California, and qualified for an architectural license through apprenticeship. He became Lomax's right-hand man and still maintains a professional relationship with the architectural legend.

For the past 20 years he has established his own practice and received much recognition as one of the bright young stars of the Southern California architectural scene. He readily admits to having one foot in the past and one foot in the future. The work of Studio Pali Fekete architects has all the sparseness of classic modernist design, yet exudes 21st-century vitality. Working within the modernist precept, the firm uses new materials in innovative ways—quietly pushing the design envelope. It's work has a worldwide presence with competition-winning designs from Egypt to China, all of it fresh and exciting.

The Nightingale house is perched high on a hill overlooking Los Angeles—not far from the iconic Hollywood sign. The neighborhood was first developed in the early 1970s by a merchant builder who placed smallish tract houses on 1,000-square-meter lots with little regard to site or environment. In the past five to six years the neighborhood has become one of L.A.'s more fashionable districts and the 1970s tract houses have given way to impressive modernist residences designed by L.A.'s leading architects.

The Nightingale house is one of three houses the firm has built on this hillside. The house is cut into the steep incline with large concrete retaining walls supporting the hill behind. The result of the cut allows for a large, flat grassy area and a house with a strong horizontal profile facing the city below. An oversized pivot-hinged door opens into a grand central hall that runs about half the length of the building. The hall is illuminated with a large skylight and terminates at a reflecting pool framed with Corten steel. The thin exterior louvers on the south and west sides of the house are

concrete boards approximately 1 centimeter wide. They filter the strong L.A. sun and provide a degree of privacy so that curtains are only needed in the bathrooms. The concrete-board louvers also add a significant 90-degree counterpoint to the building's strong horizontal elements. The floors are baked Austrian hardwood with a carved checked pattern for durability. Tucked away in a level below the main living space are a home theater, home office, guest quarters, and a wine cellar. The living room is flanked on one side by the reflecting pool and on the other by a glass wall with breathtaking city views. Although much grander in scale, the Nightingale house is reminiscent of Pierre Koenig's Case Study House #22, which is just a few miles away. It is an elegant modernist retreat, part of the city, yet floating, cloud-like, 400 meters above it.

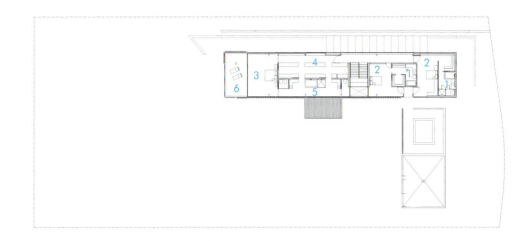

Second floor plan
1 Bathroom
2 Bedroom
3 Master bedroom
4 Master closet
5 Master bathroom
6 Deck

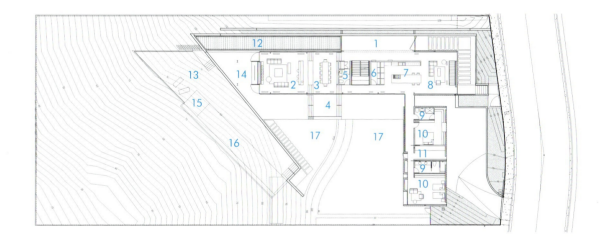

First floor plan
1 Entry
2 Living room
3 Dining room
4 Outdoor dining
5 Powder room
6 Pantry
7 Kitchen
8 Family room
9 Bathroom
10 Bedroom
11 Laundry room
12 Lily pond
13 Deck
14 Covered porch
15 Spa
16 Pool
17 Lawn

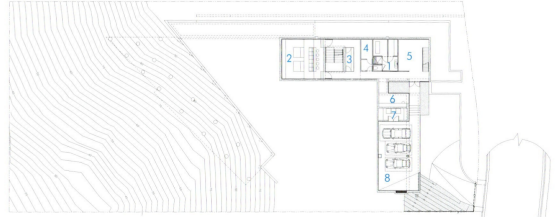

Basement floor plan
1 Bathroom
2 Theater room
3 Wine box
4 Utility/mechanical room
5 Playroom
6 Office
7 Storage
8 Garage

Hillside Houses North of San Francisco

Swatt Architects

If modernism were a religion, Robert Swatt certainly would be an acolyte. He has been lighting candles for modernism since he was 10 years old. Growing up in West Los Angeles surrounded by modern design and a pro-building environment meant that becoming an architect was his logical destiny. His grandfather was a builder and his grandmother a painter. After architectural school at the University of California in Berkeley, Swatt worked with Cesar Pelli in Los Angeles. He says every young architect in his office spent most of their time trying to squeeze the space between the glass window wall and the steel column. He on the other hand, was more interested in spending his evenings and weekends walking the hills of Hollywood and West Los Angeles looking for the hidden architectural treasures of Neutra, Gill and Schindler. Several of his early houses have the 1920s early modernist look of a Neutra or Gill.

With a new wife and young daughter, Swatt ended up back in Northern California where he opened up his own practice with Bernard Stein. He met some early success designing hillside homes in the East Bay Hills, but was soon overtaken by the postmodern craze that held sway in California and the rest of the Western world for arguably longer that it should have. In 1995 Swatt designed his own home, a strong, unabashed modernist building in one of San Francisco's eastern suburbs. The house won numerous national awards and helped establish him as a serious proponent of the modernist style in Northern California. Swatt, working closely with his partner of 20 years, Steven Stept, has become one of the pillars of modernism in the San Francisco Bay Area. Recently, he partnered with George Miers, a well-known Bay Area architect who has worked primarily in the public sector.

Garay House

Sitting on a hill overlooking San Francisco Bay, Robert Swatt must have had Richard Neutra in the back of his mind when he designed the Garay house. Set into a steep hillside, its sleek tan lines stand out against the verdant and rock-studded hills. The travertine-clad piano nobile flows seamlessly past retracting walls of glass onto agave-bordered patios and spectacular views of the bay. A narrow lap pool is like an exclamation point as it terminates at a wall of Jerusalem flagstone and the main living space. A steel moment frame is hidden carefully behind metal cladding allowing for unobstructed fenestration and 90-degree glass corners. Roof overhangs that stretch horizontally in three directions control solar heat gain and provide covered patios and decks for year-round outdoor living. The clear span glass yields ever-changing day and night vistas of the bay, the Golden Gate Bridge, and San Francisco making this Marin County hillside one of the most desirable places to live in Northern California.

The Garay's lived on this site for a number of years before they decided to do a major remodel. After a number of false starts, their modest remodel became a completely new Swatt-designed structure that expanded significantly the footprint of the original house. Strict zoning mandated that the house have a low profile on its prominent hillside site. Swatt used a handful of architectural tricks to counteract the city's height restrictions and give the interiors a bright and open feel. Pop-up clerestories and skylights bring in light from four directions and offset the intense light from the bay-side window walls. A tight entry hall steps down into an expansive piano nobile with only a subtle change in ceiling heights. Meticulous detailing, elegant materials and a soft palette of earthen hues give the house a mid-20th-century Southern-Californian look.

Hudson-Panos House

Swatt's Hudson-Panos house is far from his most upscale commission, but its strength lies in its simplicity and elegance. The 300-square-meter house sits near a hill's crest in the Sonoma wine country and is surrounded by vineyards and orchards. It is a deceivingly simple rectangle that opens on all three sides with both expansive and intimate views of vineyards and the Mayacamus Mountains. His clients are a professional couple who live in a traditional high-rise on Nob Hill in San Francisco. They wanted a weekend home that offered something completely different from their hyper-urban redoubt in the city. The house, set on an east–west axis, has intimate courtyards or decks off almost every room. The eastern entry side of the building is defined by a 15-meter cantilevered portico, which extends beyond the building giving it an almost Wright-like quality. The rear of the house has a large folding window wall that opens the kitchen completely to an outdoor eating area and a pool terrace. On the north side of the building Swatt placed a fire pit in the courtyard to provide warmth in the chill of the occasional foggy nights that blow in off the ocean a few kilometers to the west. His trademark double-volume living spaces add to the sense of openness. The ceilings in the main living space are wood-paneled, offering a visual break and a sense of warmth. The Hudson-Panos house is an uncluttered gem in California's wine country.

Second floor plan
1 Master bedroom

First floor plan
1 Living room
2 Dining room
3 Kitchen
4 Bedroom

Modernism: Elegant and Reproducible

Ray Kappe, FAIA

If modern architecture has a spiritual leader in California, it is Ray Kappe. His name solicits veneration and awe whenever it is mentioned—and for good reason. He is one of the last surviving prolific modernists from the movement's heady years of popularity in the 1950s and 1960s and he is still designing significant work today. He singlehandedly started not one, but two schools of architecture in Southern California, the California Polytechnic Institute at Pomona and the Southern California Institute of Architecture. He is, in no small way, responsible for the education of thousands of architects working throughout California. In his lifetime, he has seen modernism rise in popularity, fall from favor, and then rise again as the sought-after style.

Kappe grew up in Los Angeles and studied architecture at the University of California at Berkeley from 1947 to 1951. He started his professional life working for the prestigious modernist firm, Anshen and Allen in San Francisco. He moved back to Los Angeles after graduation and worked for Carl Maston before starting his own practice in 1953 at age 26. The 1950s was a great decade to be an architect in Southern California. The post-war boom was in full swing and a powerful wave of westward migration was afoot. Modernism, with its clean lines and open spaces, became part of the symbolic language of the era. Kappe prospered and made a name for himself. In 1968, he was asked to start the architecture department at California State Polytechnic University in Pomona, a satellite city of Los Angeles. In three and a half years, he had 350 students and a faculty of 15. In 1972, he was asked to leave over a dispute with the school administration. He did, and in the process he took with him more than half the faculty and 50 students to found a new, independent school of architecture, the Southern California Institute of Architecture, known as SCI-Arc. In a world of big ideas and big egos, Kappe managed to reign in a diverse and talented faculty and successfully lead one of the few independent schools of architecture in the United States for more than 15 years. Today, SCI-Arc graduates and faculty represent the architectural vanguard in California and the United States.

While still on the board of SCI-Arc, Kappe has devoted most of his time to lecturing and his practice. In the past few years he has become the lead architect in a prefabricated-home project called Living Homes. To date they have built two homes, with six more awaiting governmental approval. The Brentwood house is the second of the prefab series to be built by Living Homes.

The Brentwood house is a series of 4-by-16-meter factory-made steel frames that are trucked to the site and assembled on a pre-built foundation. Each module is house-specific with rough plumbing, HVAC, and electrical installed. Once assembly is complete, floors, windows, and doors are installed and electrical and plumbing finished. As any architect knows, houses are a complex integration of many individual systems. Creating a house in a factory and assembling it on a site can be a daunting task.

In theory, constructing a building in a factory makes lots of sense, but the devil is in the details. The Brentwood house's owner said that there were missteps in the fabrication that added time and expense to the process. That being said, the end result is quite spectacular.

In many ways the house is very much Ray Kappe. It has a wonderful openness that belies its factory origins. Its concrete floors, exposed steel frame and floor-to-ceiling fenestration provide the feeling of earlier Case Study Homes of Koenig and Ellwood. As with many Kappe houses, the discrete introduction of wood surfaces softens the overall harshness of steel and glass and adds a refreshing counterpoint to the overall design. Built on a steep hillside site, Kappe solved the problem of a dark rear of the house by putting together a continuous string of 45-centimeter-high clerestory windows along the entire upslope side of the building. The second story bridges over the first and allows for an unenclosed section of hillside that serves as a light well and hidden garden for the first-floor bedrooms. A spacious roof deck spans the entire second story, allowing ample room for entertaining or just reading the Sunday paper.

Prefab houses may need to undergo a series of iterations before they become part of the more universally accepted building techniques, but Kappe's contribution proves once and for all that prefab homes needn't be ugly nor boring copies of stick-built houses.

Second floor plan
1. Breakfast room
2. Kitchen
3. Dining room
4. Mechanical
5. Media
6. Living room
7. Deck
8. Powder room

First floor plan
1. Entry
2. Bedroom
3. Bathroom
4. Master bedroom
5. Master closet
6. Master bathroom
7. Laundry

URBAN LIVING

2

A House of Steel for a Man of Glass in West Berkeley

Regan Bice Architects

Regan Bice lives and works in a gritty, industrial part of Berkeley known more for its patchwork pattern of warehouses, small factories, and blue-collar housing than for the elegant townhouses on tree-lined streets that surround the university a few kilometers to the east. He has been an active part of a new urbanism that has quietly transformed blighted cities and neighborhoods along the coast of California from San Diego to Eureka, much of it with a 21st-century modernist style that would make Le Corbusier smile. His projects use industrial materials and shapes in refined and elegant ways.

Bice's journey towards modern architecture, and indeed to California, was circumambulatory at best. He grew up in Michigan and Connecticut, and went to school in Wisconsin majored in economics, although he always had an interest in architecture. He attended architecture school for a short time before military draft problems forced him to leave the United States in the 1970s. He ended up in Menorca, Spain helping his sister remodel a house there. He was hired by a British company to design vacation homes for British citizens and northern Europeans who wanted a place in the Spanish sun. He left that position after a short time and started his own firm with Bay Area architect and friend, Phillip Matthews. He eventually partnered with another Spanish architect and actively worked in Spain for seven years, completing numerous projects in Menorca and Barcelona before returning to the United States. Bice ended up in San Francisco where he landed a position with an engineering firm who had the commission to remodel the entire cable-car system. His work transitioned from restoring villas in Spain to trolley barns in San Francisco. He eventually acquired enough credits to qualify for a license, passed the exam and opened his own practice in Berkeley in 1988. Once again, he was designing villas, only this time in costal California. Bice's work is thoroughly modern in both urban and suburban environments. Stucco, married with corrugated metal and stainless sheath, provides pristine, well-proportioned, eye-catching volumes.

The Lipofsky house is a good example of an industrial aesthetic turned residential. West Berkeley has long been a mix of working-class residences and light industry. Artists and musicians have lived next to warehouses and factories for generations. Marvin Lipofsky is one of the world's leading glass artists. When not lecturing or working in Eastern Europe or Asia, Lipofsky calls Berkeley his home. He has taught at the University of California, Berkeley and California College of Arts in the adjacent city of Oakland for a number of years. For most of that time, he and his artist wife lived in his studio in West Berkeley. They acquired the land next to their existing studio and commissioned Bice, a neighbor, to build them a new house.

Bice came up with a plan to build two town homes connected by a garage and roof deck on one lot. Mirroring the industrial look of many of the surrounding structures, Bice clad the almost symmetrical units in corrugated aluminum and stainless steel. The buildings rise

three stories to the maximum height limit, but step back on the top floor leaving room for roof decks with views of San Francisco Bay. The units have slightly different programs. Marvin's first story is a gallery and office space and his wife's third story is a studio, but they enclose similar volumes and connect on the second floor with a deck and on the third with a continuous roof banded in B2 stainless steel. The effect ties the two buildings together and creates a continuous massing of the third story. At first glance, the building's appearance gives the impression of a very cool office or industrial space. But on closer examination, it is clear that this is a residence for people who are quite fond of the industrial look. The quiet, minimalist interiors provide ample space for their significant collections of artworks and objets d'art.

Regan Bice's genius is revealed by his ability to integrate the modernist aesthetic with the industrial in urban infill projects. His West Berkeley projects are stellar examples of 21st-century California-style urban living.

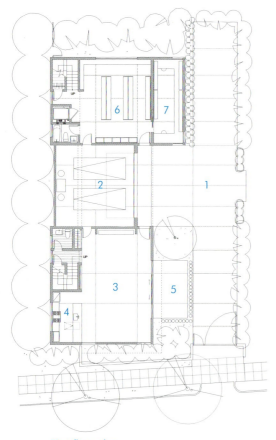

First floor plan
1. Driveway
2. Shared garage
3. Unit 1: living space
4. Unit 1: kitchen
5. Unit 1: terrace
6. Unit 2: art display
7. Unit 2: office

Second floor plan
1. Unit 1: office
2. Unit 1: master bedroom
3. Unit 1: master bathroom
4. Shared covered deck
5. Shared storage
6. Unit 2: living space
7. Unit 2: library

Third floor plan
1. Unit 1: studio
2. Unit 1: deck
3. Unit 2: master bedroom
4. Unit 2: master bathroom
5. Unit 2: deck

Big City Architect, Big City House

Johnson Fain

Scott Johnson is a man for all seasons. He is a California native who studied at two of the nation's premier architectural schools, Berkeley and Harvard. He has worked extensively on both coasts with some of the leading architects of the day. Trained as a modernist at Berkeley and Harvard, he worked for Johnson Burgee in New York City during the height of their postmodern period designing some of the detailing on the groundbreaking AT&T building. In the early 1980s he was asked to join the legendary Southern California firm of William Pereira & Associates and his longtime friend from Harvard, William Fain, who had migrated west several years earlier. Soon Johnson and Fain found themselves running the firm.

Johnson Fain has successfully transitioned from the postmodern period to a modernist style, designing large-scale projects across the United States and East Asia. Johnson admits that he initially regretted moving from the intimacy of New York to the vast, horizontal, and seemingly empty spaces of Los Angeles, but he learned to adapt and since thrived. Spending most of his life in or near big cities, he has come to appreciate the urbanity of Los Angeles, subtle as it is. He brings an intellectual presence to architecture that is rarely found outside academia and uses this approach in much of his design work. His home library has several thousand volumes, mostly on architecture, and it is apparent that he has read most of them. His distinguished demeanor and "Corbu" glasses would be at home on any college campus.

For architects, the exercise of designing one's own house provides license to experiment with a variety of design ideas and materials that may be outside the taste of the average client. The Larchmont house is no exception. Built in a commercial district in Hancock Park, Los Angeles, Larchmont neither clashes with its neighbors nor completely blends in. From the street, it could be a small office building or one very cool house. Once inside, however, there is no mistaking that this is a well lived in and inviting family residence. The house sits on a first-story pedestal that is reserved for parking and utilities. A central open steel staircase leads to the second story and primary living spaces. The living room projects out with a trapezoidal bay overlooking a tight, urban garden and busy Larchmont Boulevard. It makes a strong statement about being in the heart of the city. The other major rooms on the main level look inward around an internal courtyard with a square swimming pool and striking colored Plexiglas sculpture that helps define the space and project color into the adjacent rooms. The courtyard provides a place of daily solitude and a great outdoor venue for social gatherings. The master bedroom at the rear of the main floor is a circular, womb-like room painted a burnt sienna hue. Johnson's wife, an obstetrician, necessarily keeps unconventional hours and therefore needs an environment that aids sleep, even on a busy city street. The living room and hallways are lined with bookshelves housing Johnson's extensive design library. The third story contains an office library in a 270-degree glass drum, brilliantly illuminated by translucent floor-to-ceiling glass panels. At night, the library becomes something of a beacon on Larchmont Boulevard, signaling that good architecture is alive and well in West Los Angeles.

Third floor plan
1 Bedroom
2 Study

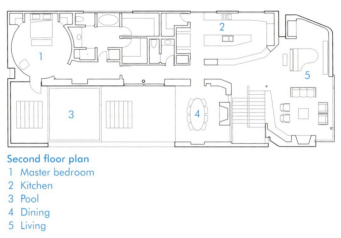

Second floor plan
1 Master bedroom
2 Kitchen
3 Pool
4 Dining
5 Living

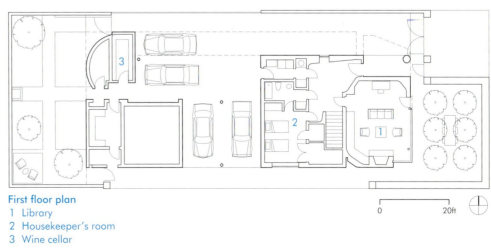

First floor plan
1 Library
2 Housekeeper's room
3 Wine cellar

111

Modernism, San Francisco Style

Craig Steely Architecture

Craig Steely is not your typical architect. He has danced around the profession wearing a variety of hats for almost 20 years. In that time, he has been a builder, a set and window-display designer, a furniture designer and an architect. Today he maintains an active practice in San Francisco and the Big Island of Hawaii. He has developed a reputation as one of California's most innovative young architects.

Steely grew up on a ranch in the foothills of the Sierra Nevada mountain range, where he was always building and fixing things. Ranch life meant that nothing was thrown away—they would just find a new use for it. After high school he moved to the ski-resort area of Bear Valley where he worked winters on the ski slopes and summers in construction. That led to an interest in architecture, which in turn led to a professional degree from California Polytechnic University, San Luis Obispo. His thesis year in college was spent studying in Italy with Cristiano Toraldo di Francia, formerly of Superstudio. He says he loved Italy and never would have left except that he met his future wife there, who just happened to be a San Franciscan studying abroad. They returned to California in 1990, a time of significant economic downturn. Steely worked for Jim Jennings for a short time before starting his own design practice. The last 10 or so years have been productive ones for Steely, having completed work on over 30 projects in Northern California and the Island of Hawaii. These days, he works out of his Upper Market Street studio in San Francisco, where he lives with his wife and son. He says he loves living and working in his compact, intensely urban, multiethnic neighborhood and finds himself doing a fair amount of design work very close to home. In a city known for its stately Victorian and classical row houses, Steely's modernist infill houses certainly stand out, but manage not to clash with their neighbors. They exude an almost 1950s retro modernism, but have enough individuality and innovation to be unmistakably 21st-century designs.

Xiao-Yen's house fits this description. Xiao-Yen is a feature-film director whose frank, award-winning films about China and the United States are not approved for screening by the Chinese government. As a consequence, she lives in San Francisco, shoots in China and distributes her films to the international community outside the Peoples' Republic.

The site is on one of San Francisco's lesser-known hills in the heart of the city, bordered by a park. A Victorian from the late 19th century once stood there, ravaged by termites, earthquakes, fires, and poorly executed remodels. Little was savable. In its place Steely designed a compact, vertical house with stacked working and living quarters and a top-story redwood-paneled study and surrounding roof garden. For seismic reasons, the house required a significant moment frame. Steely accomplished this by designing an exoskeleton steel frame. The main staircase is hung on this frame, along with decks and a bi-facial solar panel array that supplies most of the electricity consumed by the house. The exoskeleton also supports the upper floor creating a column-free room with a view. San Francisco's lots are long and narrow mandating houses with similarly shaped floor plans. Steely compensated for this with an open plan and a large skylight over the kitchen.

Xiao-Yen's husband and partner, Andy Martin, is an accomplished artist and sculptor. He had collected more than 40 years worth of redwood scraps and he wanted Steely to incorporate them into the project. Steely's solution was to rip the tailings into five unique sizes and then randomly attach them in varying combinations, much in the fashion of a Louise Nevelson sculpture, to create the house's façade. A whitewash finish was applied to protect the wood. From a distance, the façade has a uniform appearance, but a delicate and intricate pattern of shadows and highlights is revealed close-up.

San Francisco is a compact, intensely urban environment with a spectacular maritime setting and a rich architectural history. Building anything new can be a challenge. Steely is in some ways a latter-day urban pioneer creating eye-catching projects that manage to successfully weave themselves into the city's urban fabric.

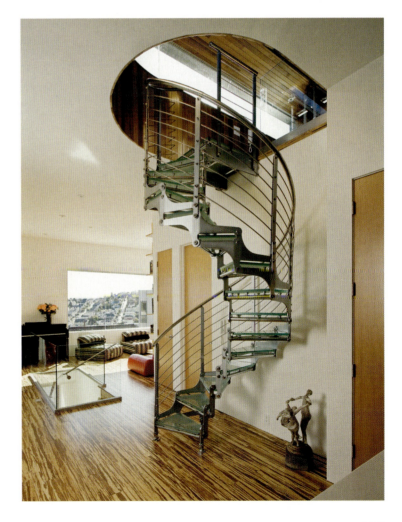

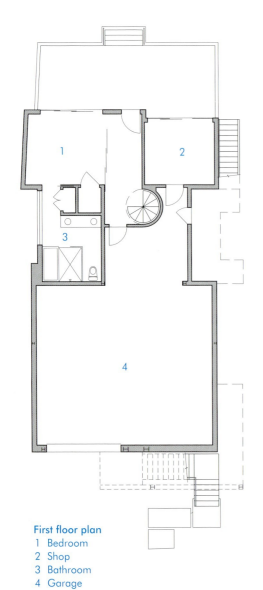

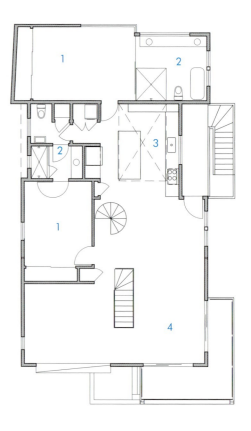

First floor plan
1 Bedroom
2 Shop
3 Bathroom
4 Garage

Second floor plan
1 Living
2 Dining
3 Bathroom
4 Laundry
5 Kitchen
6 Bedroom
7 Office

Third floor plan
1 Bedroom
2 Bathroom
3 Kitchen
4 Living

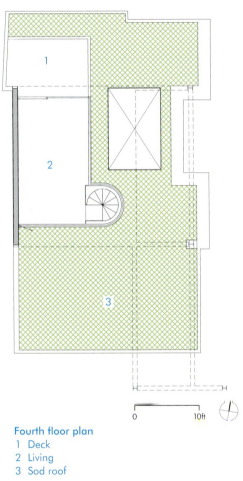

Fourth floor plan
1 Deck
2 Living
3 Sod roof

119

A Line from Craig Ellwood to the Present

Macy Architecture

Mark Macy is inspired by Craig Ellwood's engineering and design legacy. Many of his projects exhibit the same design rigor and engineering concepts so emblematic in Ellwood's work from the mid 20th century. Ellwood was, above all, a pragmatic engineer who saw his buildings as defined by their structure. It was the exposed steel perimeter moment frame that became his trademark. Whatever function or design happened with the building happened inside its exoskeleton of steel. "Structure is the only clear principle," Ellwood said. Macy, more than most 21st-century modernists, has followed this dictum in his work. His practice covers a broad spectrum of building genres, from commercial and institutional work to residences, but the legacy of Ellwood's discipline is always there.

Mark Macy's architectural lineage reaches back at least one generation. His father was an architect in San Diego, where he was instrumental in the establishment of the city's historic Gas Lamp Quarter. Macy knew he was going to be an architect from a very young age. He studied architecture at California Polytechnic University at San Luis Obispo and furthered his architectural studies with Cristiano Toraldo di Francia, one of the founders of Superstudio, in Florence, Italy. He loved Italy, but soon realized that he needed to find his architectural future back in California. He landed in Los Angeles, but found it a little too car-centric for his taste. He migrated north and found work in the San Francisco Bay Area with Fernau and Hartman, a well-known critical-regionalist architectural firm. He stayed there for nine years before starting his own practice in San Francisco. His work covers a wide variety of building types, from schools to retail to houses, and is always interesting. His residential work, however, is where he is most free to express his core concepts of structure and form.

Macy drew from his Italian experiences when he designed the Point Loma house in San Diego. Sitting on a slight rise with commanding ocean views, the house is part of an existing city neighborhood of 1920s cottages and 1950s ranchers. The extra-wide lot permitted Macy to give the house a strong horizontal shape parallel to the street. In the Point Loma house, Macy utilizes the design concepts of Palladio (the 16th-century classicist) and Ellwood (the 20th-century modernist) in articulating its form and function. Inside the Ellwood-inspired steel perimeter moment frame is a very classical, nine-square Palladian house plan. The main living space is on the second floor. An impressive double-height entry hall with a grand piano occupies the first floor with symmetrical adjacent spaces relegated to secondary bedrooms and a game room. The second floor is also laid out in symmetrical fashion with the main living area on one side and the master bedroom suite and office on the other. Only an offset entry portico and dramatically cantilevered deck break the symmetry. Behind the main house is a garage and woodshop building that is connected by a breezeway. A miniature orchard of fruit trees and a *karesansui*, a raked gravel Zen garden, separate the two buildings. The house also incorporates passive-solar and natural-ventilation design principles. Horizontal sunshades are sized to shield glass from the summer sun while allowing winter sun. The interior is naturally ventilated via the central atrium and

clerestory windows. The steel-frame house is sheathed in 10-millimeter composite phenolic-wood panels with air space behind to mitigate heat gain. Photovoltaic arrays on the flat roof generate almost all of the house's energy. Irrigation is provided by rainwater collected from the roofs and stored in underground cisterns.

Despite its strong geometry and classical layout, the Point Loma house offers unexpected warmth and openness. A translucent glass fence on the house's street side creates a bright, intimate, private garden that can be enjoyed year-round in San Diego's mild climate. In a culturally conservative seaside town, Mark Macy has reinvented classical modernism for the 21st century.

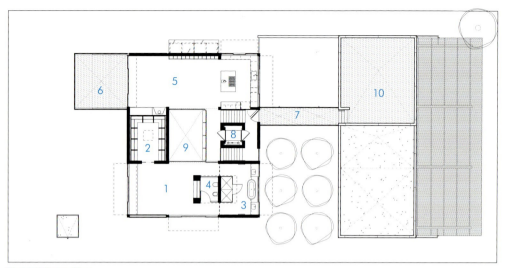

Second floor plan
1. Master bedroom
2. Master closet
3. Master bathroom
4. Restroom
5. Living/dining/kitchen
6. Cantilevered deck
7. Bridge
8. Elevator
9. Atrium
10. View terrace

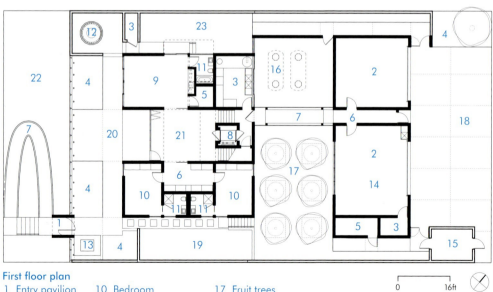

First floor plan
1. Entry pavilion
2. Garage
3. Utility
4. Planter
5. Storage closet
6. Hall
7. Ramp
8. Elevator
9. Family room
10. Bedroom
11. Bathroom
12. Spa
13. Water feature
14. Workshop
15. Trash/recycling
16. Zen garden/ underground rainwater cisterns
17. Fruit trees
18. Carport
19. Vegetable/herb garden
20. Entry patio
21. Entry atrium
22. Native grasses/ California poppy
23. Artificial lawn

127

Two Venetian Cousins

Callas Shortridge architects

In some ways, Callas and Shortridge can be thought of as "the odd couple" of architecture. Barbara Callas is precise, demanding and in control while Steven has a more devil-may-care approach. The end result is an architectural practice that turns out project after project exuding both creativity and precision. No two projects look alike, yet each one manages to redefine modernism without resorting to standard design clichés. Both Callas and Shortridge were partners with Frank Israel in the mid 1990s. Israel, a bright light and innovator in the architecture scene of Southern California, set a high bar for creativity. Israel's vast and varied architectural skills spanned from set design to private homes, to university buildings. When Israel died prematurely in 1996, his aesthetic legacy was handed over to Callas and Shortridge, who have carried the torch ever since.

Steven Shortridge was raised in Kentucky and got his first architectural degree from Texas A&M. His father was an engineer who built their first house when Steven was five years old. From that point on he saw architecture as his destiny. He worked in Dallas for three years before studying at Massachusetts Institute of Technology in Cambridge. With a professional degree in hand, he was drawn to the two cultural poles of the United States, New York, and Los Angeles. He chose Los Angeles and has not looked back.

Barbara Callas was born and raised in the high desert of California about an hour east of Los Angeles. Her family lived next to Edwards Air Force Base and NASA. Her classmates were the children of men and women working on the U.S. space program and other experimental aviation projects. Callas says her childhood career ambition was to be a test pilot, but she soon discovered that designing and building things was more fun than flying them. At the University of California, Los Angeles, Callas earned a degree in product design (UCLA did not have an undergraduate program in architecture at this point in time). She returned later to complete a graduate degree in architecture. It was at UCLA that she met Israel, one of her professors. Callas's design skills impressed Israel and he invited her to join his firm. Her construction knowledge, design innovation and the fact that she was a licensed architect prompted Israel to make her a partner. After his death, Callas and Shortridge took over the firm. Callas Shortridge has continued to be one of L.A.'s most creative, boutique architectural firms.

543 House

The 543 House in Venice was originally a spec building project. Callas and Shortridge bought the land, did the original design work, and permitted the job. Shortridge found a buyer who added some changes and asked for numerous upgrades. The net result was a positive transformation.

The 543 House is a deceptive, yet very clever house. From the street, it looks like two gray boxes hidden behind a translucent fence and some lush landscaping. Once inside the front door, a very different experience unfolds. Large, voluminous spaces stack one upon another at half-floor intervals creating the illusion of a huge house—all this on a half lot measuring 10 by 24 meters.

The 543 House is also an exercise in verticality. A central open staircase rises through seven levels from the alley-side garage to the roof deck, offering vistas on each half floor of the levels above and below. On the ground floor, ceiling-high glass doors open up to a postage-stamp front yard backed with a Corten steel wall and gas-powered fireplace, perfect for parties on summer evenings when the chilling fog rolls in off the Pacific. The dining room is flanked by the living room on the level above and the kitchen on the level below. The living room, which has a large flat-panel TV and a sophisticated sound system, can be turned into a screening room easily, an important feature for the owner, a TV producer. As with all of Callas Shortridge's work, attention to detail is everywhere. Wood-paneled walls miter perfectly. Corian countertops wrap at 90 degrees and become walls or counter legs. The master bath blends cantilevered Corian vanities with hardwood veneer cabinetry and dark tile in a delicate interplay of volumes and surfaces. Venice, a neighborhood of seaside cottages and elegant townhouses, has a noteworthy addition to its architectural patchwork.

Dunn Moray House

Scott Dunn and Robbie Moray are two guys on the go. Scott is a concert pianist and conductor of orchestras on two coasts. Robbie has a growing fashion business, Illia, and his clothes are sold in high-end boutiques around the country. Dunn and Moray had lived high in one of Los Angeles' remote canyons, but wanted to be closer to the heart of the city. Shortridge found them a "tear down" on a lot in Venice just blocks from the ocean and the main shopping street. The lot was full sized, with both street and alley access. This permitted Shortridge to design a house that took full advantage of its long and narrow dimensions. Just as the 543 House was an exercise in verticality, the Dunn Moray house is its horizontal cousin. As with many of Callas and Shortridge's designs, its street presence reveals little of what is inside. Working with associate David Spinelli, who did much of the detail design work, Shortridge wrapped three horizontal volumes around an internal courtyard defined by a lap pool and an enclosed patio. Each volume defines a function (public, private, and studio) and has its own unique quality. The primary exterior sheathing is 10-millimeter concrete panels screwed on to metal channels. Spinelli turned these panels horizontally and made them the interior ceiling for much of the first floor (the public volume). The hall, running the length of the first-floor volume, is bordered by a glass wall that conveniently rolls away giving seamless access to the courtyard and pool. Scott has two Steinway grand pianos in the house. One sits in a niche off the living room and the other resides in his music studio situated above the garage and at the rear of the house. The pianos do not sit idle. When not in New York, Scott is busy in this studio preparing for his next concert. The studio has a private second-floor deck that offers filtered views of the nearby Pacific.

Tucked between a vacant lot and a 1920s cottage on a quiet Venice street, the Dunn Moray house makes a welcome statement about modernism and urbanism in ever-changing L.A.

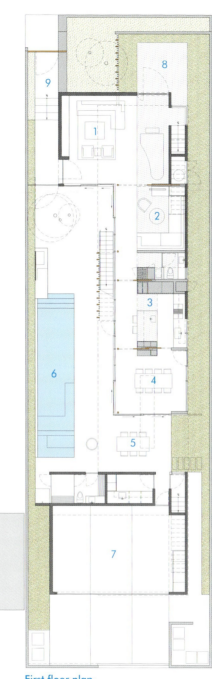

First floor plan
1. Living room
2. Family room
3. Kitchen
4. Dining room
5. Outdoor seating
6. Pool
7. 3-car garage
8. Front deck
9. Entrance (front)

Second floor plan
1. Master bathroom
2. Master bedroom
3. Office
4. Guest room
5. Deck
6. Studio and office

0   10ft

3

BEACH HOUSES

The House is a (Recycled) Machine for Living

David Hertz Architects Inc., Studio of Environmental Architecture

David Hertz is a Southern California boy. He says he always wanted to be an architect and seems to have taken the right steps. After graduating from SCI-Arc, the avant-garde architectural school founded by Ray Kappe, he went to work for John Lautner, one of the legendary modernists of the 1950s. After leaving Lautner, he worked for Frank Gehry for a number of years before starting his own practice. Materials have always been a key interest for Hertz. He developed a type of lightweight concrete using recycled materials and pioneered the use of concrete countertops and decorative tiles. Going green has been a large part of Hertz' design work from the beginning. Many of his projects involve recycled materials, some in very unique ways.

The Panel house on Los Angeles' Venice beach sits on a slim lot wedged between other beachfront houses. Like spectators at a parade rope line—some fat, some tall—all sit in anticipation of the show before it. The show, of course, is the pedestrian promenade, the beach and the Pacific Ocean as the infinite backdrop. All day long, people stroll, rollerblade, or bicycle along the pedestrian path that separates the houses from the beach. They provide a continuous people-watching show that is rich with eccentricity, humor, and old-fashioned family life. Having a picture window on Venice Beach is somewhat like having your own 8-meter-wide flat-screen TV that plays a reality show of L.A. life 24/7.

With the Panel house, Hertz has given new meaning to Le Corbusier's famous dictum, "The house is a machine for living in." With the Panel house, this "machine" uses recycled materials as a major building component. The wall panels are the same as those used to make industrial refrigeration buildings. They have foam inserts, are skinned with aluminum and painted dull metallic silver. The panels fit into a muscular steel frame that articulates itself throughout the building. The house stacks up three-plus stories from street level to roof deck, connected by an open steel staircase and open industrial elevator. Light wells and skylights illuminate the core of the building while expansive window walls open out to the ocean views. The house's owner is a well-known inventor and entrepreneur. As a consequence, the house contains numerous technologically innovative building conventions not found elsewhere. For example, the entire front window opens vertically, giving a truly unobstructed view of the beach and ocean. The living-room fireplace is a small pile of shattered tempered glass with a concealed natural gas source and sits conveniently under the large flat-panel TV suspended on cables. Passersby strolling the promenade are greeted by a compact waterfall that shimmers over a low retaining wall and is topped by a 30-by-50-centimeter piece of grass the owner has dubbed the "world's smallest front yard." The owner, a man with a rich sense of humor, relishes both his public persona and access to the ocean. If public display is something of a religion in L.A., Venice Beach is its holy city and the Panel house could easily be considered its newest temple.

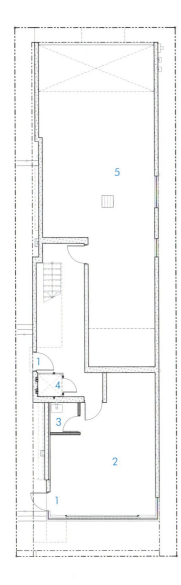
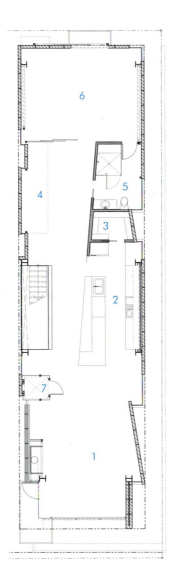
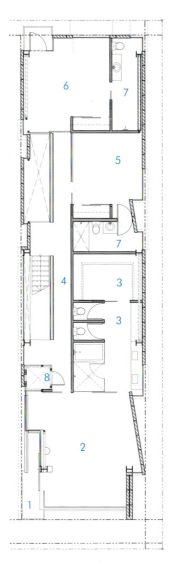
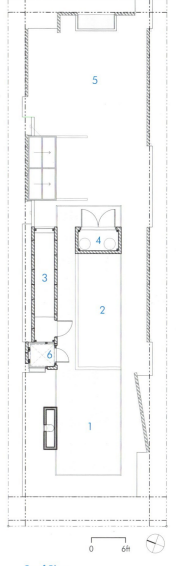

First floor plan
1 Beach entry
2 Guest bedroom
3 Guest/beach bathroom
4 Elevator
5 Garage

Second floor plan
1 Living room
2 Kitchen
3 Pantry
4 Dining
5 Bathroom
6 Media room
7 Elevator

Third floor plan
1 Master balcony
2 Master bedroom
3 Master bathroom/closet
4 Hallway
5 Bedroom
6 Bedroom
7 Bathroom
8 Elevator

Roof Plan
1 Roof deck
2 Swim-in-place pool
3 Stairwell
4 Mechanical
5 Photovoltaic solar array
6 Elevator

150

153

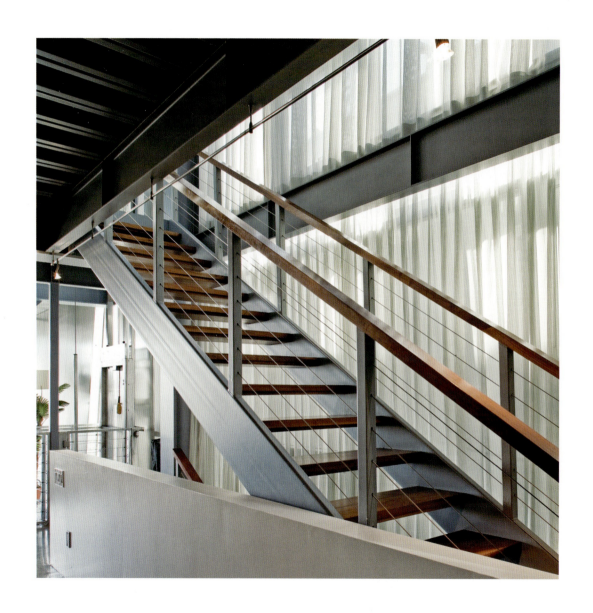

Beach Town Houses, North and South

Ehrlich Architects

Steven Ehrlich is a warm and funny guy. Easily approachable, he seems without the pretences or remoteness that is characteristic of some of his peers. His charm is more reminiscent of a politician than an architect. Yet that is what he is. He knows his craft and is a master of it. His buildings have an individuality and polish that is unique. In the firmament of the City of Angels he has found a place as one of its brighter stars.

Steven Ehrlich knew his destiny from an early age. His father was an engineer and inventor and instilled in Steven the desire to tinker and create. At 12 he designed a solar house that won first prize at the New Jersey State Fair. He was hooked. He went on to study architecture at Rensselaer Polytechnic Institute in upstate New York. After graduating he joined the United States Peace Corps. He was recruited as its first architect and sent to Marrakesh, Morocco, where he worked in a local government bureau for two years. Africa seems to have rubbed off on him, because he didn't go home, at least not right away. He landed a teaching position at a university in Nigeria and stayed another four years. Ehrlich says that living and working as an architect in Africa left a lasting impression on him. He learned to understand the world of "architecture without architects," a concept not clearly understood by most Westerners. It was a concept that he would bring home and later incorporate in his work in novel ways.

Returning to the United States, he paid a social call on his sister, who was living in Los Angeles. He was smitten with the mild weather and the free and easy lifestyle of Southern Californians. New Jersey became a past tense. California was the place for him to hang his professional hat.

The walls of Ehrlich's office are lined with scores of awards and citations that his firm has won over the past 25 years. California has certainly been good for him. His firm does a mix of commercial and institutional work in California and around the world, but it still maintains an active residential studio with partner Takashi Yanai, AIA. Ehrlich describes his work as "Multicultural Modernism" with liberal references to his African experiences. It is hard to categorize Ehrlich's work because each project is so different. Featured here are two projects, both from beach towns, one north and one south, with radically different looks that illustrate how Ehrlich is a modernist who is constantly pushing the architectural envelope.

700 Palms: An Architectural Oasis

One could say that 700 Palms is a steel box. One could say it is a Bedouin tent in the North African desert or a house turned inside out. In fact, all of these descriptions would have some validity. It is a house where the inside and outside blend together in simple but dramatic ways. It is a house where large volumes are juxtaposed with intimate spaces and inviting garden views. It is an urban house on a busy Los Angeles street that becomes an oasis. Simple in its design and elegant in its execution, the house demonstrates Ehrlich's use of industrial materials to create a breathtaking environment that challenges assumptions about what a house should be.

As with many of Ehrlich's houses, 700 Palms uses the entire lot with two buildings set at either end of the property. Gardens, outdoor living spaces, and a lap pool fill every square meter in between. The perimeter is defined by a 2-meter-high translucent fence that keeps the public out, but backlights the desert-motif gardens and pool area. In the main living space, a concrete block wall rises 5 meters and becomes the spine of the house and its defining interior surface. Steel and wood framing hang off the wall and support the rest of the main building. A box-like volume clad in Corten steel plate defines the street

First floor plan
1. Entry
2. Powder room
3. Dining
4. Living
5. Kitchen
6. Garage
7. Laundry
8. Storage
9. Pool

Mezzanine floor plan
1. Living
2. Bathroom
3. Deck
4. Bedroom
5. Bridge

Second floor plan
1. Library
2. Closet
3. Master bathroom
4. Laundry
5. Master bedroom
6. Deck
7. Kitchenette
8. Living
9. Bathroom

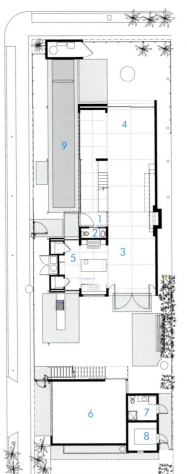

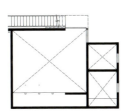

161

side of the building. Ehrlich takes the Corten steel exterior and brings it into the main living space, thereby repeating the indoor–outdoor theme.

The steel frame extends outside the building shell almost to the edge of the property line. Brightly colored retractable fabric awnings hanging on the frame give the exterior a tent-like feel. On either end of the main living space floor-to-ceiling glass walls either roll away or swing open to small gardens or patios. The indoor–outdoor transition becomes seamless and dramatic. The bedrooms and upper floors are accessed by a staircase and a vertiginous steel-and-glass bridge that hangs from the ceiling in the main space on thin steel rods. With upper rooms opening into it, the main space has a Piranesi-like quality.

Ehrlich, both a world traveler and collector, has filled the house with art and artifacts from his many overseas adventures. The steel walls in his kitchen become a ready surface for his large collection of refrigerator magnets and family snapshots. The Palms house is an exceptional work of architecture and a family home for Ehrlich and his wife, Nancy Griffin. It is one more hidden landmark in a beach town filled with interesting and provocative architecture.

Zeidler House: A Big City House for a Sleepy Central Coast Town

Ehrlich was asked to create a very different kind of beach townhouse in this sleepy hamlet on Monterey Bay. The clients, a retired couple with grown children, wanted a public house on a city street with an ocean view. The clients said they hired Ehrlich because of his interest in commissioning a purely modernist house. Ehrlich's solution was to place two buildings, one public and one private, at either end of a corner lot, separated by a sculpture garden and a pool. The public building opens boldly onto the street with floor-to-ceiling fenestration affording sweeping ocean views. The private building faces a garden and the rear of the public building.

Views out and in are all part of the design. Because of height restrictions, the house has a subterranean level that contains a large wine cellar, a TV room, and utility spaces. The master bedroom suite is on the second floor above the kitchen and dining room. Its sliding glass window and cozy deck faces the ocean and street below. A steel-framed staircase connects all three levels and sits in a metal-clad tower that runs up the rear of the main building. From the rear of the main house, a sliding glass wall opens onto the approximately 12-by-12-meter patio, providing an ample enclosed outdoor space for entertaining and outdoor living.

Ehrlich and Yanai use Reinzink panels, glass, polished concrete block, and stucco to define each of the house's exterior volumes. They cut out corner windows on each of the volumes to give them transparency and lightness. The interplay of surface textures, fenestration, and volumes is modernism at its best. On a street of upscale yet traditional modern houses, the Zeidler house is an attention-getting breath of fresh air.

Third floor plan
1 Elevator
2 Roof deck

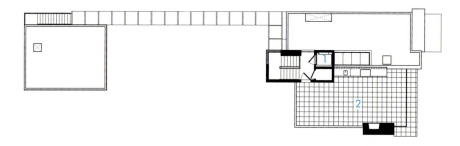

Second floor plan
1 Bathroom
2 Studio
3 Master bathroom
4 Closet
5 Master bedroom
6 Balcony
7 Elevator
8 Dressing room
9 Mezzanine
10 Open to below

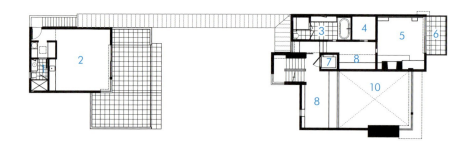

First floor plan
1 Garage
2 Bathroom
3 Guest room
4 Outdoor patio
5 Pool
6 Powder room
7 Pantry
8 Kitchen
9 Dining
10 Elevator
11 Entry
12 Family room
13 Pétanque court

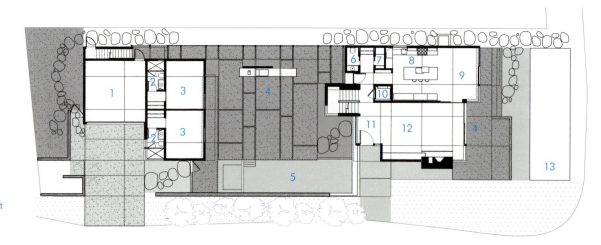

Basement floor plan
1 Laundry
2 Mechanical
3 Storage
4 Elevator
5 Wine room

Life on the Water

Seidel Architects

Living on the water has always been part of Alexander Seidel's life. Growing up in Wisconsin, his family always managed to live by a lake. His family also had a passion for architecture: one of his earliest memories is living in a Frank Lloyd Wright house in Milwaukee. He says being an architect must have been part of his DNA, citing a penchant for drawing houses as early as the first grade. His love of building led him to the Architecture School at Cornell University in upstate New York where his passion for architecture was sated. At Cornell he took classes with Colin Rowe and was introduced to the concept of contextual architecture, which made a strong counter position to the prevailing modernist design paradigms of Mies and Corbusier. He subsequently went on to Harvard's Graduate School of Design and studied architectural theory.

Immediately out of college, Seidel landed a job in San Francisco with Skidmore, Owings & Merrill (SOM), working on large-scale urban projects. Seidel was once again living next to water at his newfound home by the San Francisco Bay. He went from SOM to several other architectural firms that focused on housing and urban design before he opened his own firm with his then wife and partner, Stacy Holzman.

Most of Seidel's professional life has been spent designing high-density housing. He has created scores of apartment and condominium projects all over California. When it came time to design his personal residence, he decided that he wanted to live on the water once again.

San Francisco Bay is a large body of water with a land frontage that has been abused by industry and commerce for more than a century. Major shipping terminals and old industrial facilities line its shores in many spots. The town of Tiburon is in Marin County, north of San Francisco was a rail terminus until the 1950s, when better roads and the Golden Gate Bridge obviated the need for a rail terminus. Tiburon went from a blue-collar shipping terminal to a suburb almost overnight. The train tracks were pulled out and the low-lying marshland was reclaimed to create new bay-front communities. The adjacent Belvedere Lagoon was one of those newly minted urban reclamation environs. In addition to merchant builders, individuals hired noted Bay Area modernist architects to design dream homes on the water. Protected by locks and levies, the lagoon became an oasis on the bay that few knew about.

Second floor plan
1 Bedroom
2 Office

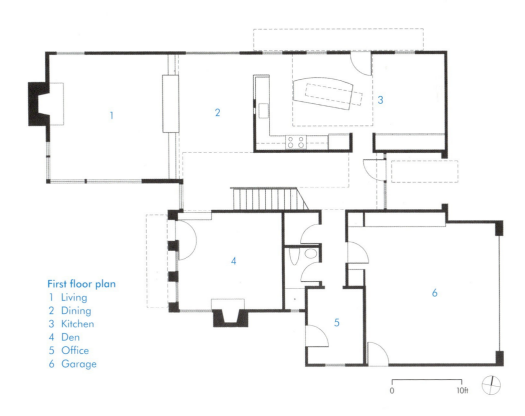

First floor plan
1 Living
2 Dining
3 Kitchen
4 Den
5 Office
6 Garage

The house that previously occupied the lot where Seidel built his house was a ramshackle affair of unknown pedigree. It came down quickly. The remaining lot was small and the coverage requirements restrictive. Seidel designed his new house to take advantage of the site by orienting it toward the bay while giving the street a limited view. The house is actually not large, but the vertical volumes in the main living spaces create the illusion of a much larger one. The red cedar siding has a gray weathered finish that is somewhat evocative of the original fishing shanties that dotted the edge of the bay 50 years before. The house's simple design may be seen as an evolution of what local mid-century modernists like Esherick and Anshen were doing in the 1950s and 1960s. In fact, a number of their houses can be found on the same lagoon. The elegance of Seidel's house is in its simplicity, two volumes broken by sunshades and a flue. The main living space opens onto a tight patio and garden, which is terminated by a boat dock and the lagoon.

The shoreline of San Francisco Bay rolls on for miles, some of it industrial and commercial and much of it undisturbed tidelands, but precious little has been devoted to single-family housing. The Belvedere Lagoon house takes full advantage of its bayside site, giving its owners a modernist waterside oasis enjoyed by few in the intensely urban San Francisco Bay Area.

Beachside Fun

Studio 9 one 2

The ocean is a compelling magnet that attracts a wide variety of characters. The fog and breezes that roll off the Pacific breathe air into the lungs of Los Angeles, and most people who live in Southern California gravitate to this. "Why live in California, if you can't live next to the beach?" asks Pat Killen.

Hermosa Beach, where Killen practices under the moniker Studio 9 one 2, is one of a handful of beach towns that dot the coast just south of Los Angeles. These small towns developed near the turn of the previous century were originally summer resorts for Southern Californians. The relentless suburban growth of the city of Los Angeles in the last half of the 20th century enveloped these towns, but they still manage to maintain their quirky small-town resort character. Killen started his westward trek in Ohio where he completed his undergraduate studies at Kent State University. He migrated west, opened an office in Los Angeles and for a number of years ran a conventional architectural practice that focused on government, institutional, and commercial projects.

As with many architects who develop a large practice only to become dissatisfied, Killen closed his downtown office, moved to the beach and began working for a very different client base. Today Killen's practice revolves around serving the needs of the beach towns he has become so intimate with. Clients come to Killen when they are looking for striking, one-off architecture that reflects a master's hand. His buildings are handsome, well crafted, and iconic. They integrate geometric forms in ways that are daring, playful, and very Southern Californian.

The site 139 Hermosa Avenue is on a commercial strip in the somewhat less-posh side of Hermosa Beach. Its neighbors are a tobacco shop, a laundromat, a sushi bar, and a couple of cafés. It is a mere 25 meters from one of the prettiest stretches of beaches in Southern California. Zoning allowed for one commercial space and one residential unit above, although the site could have supported more. Killen's task was to create an eye-catching façade on a busy street corner in a commercial district that serves both residential and commercial users. His solution was a blue mosaic-clad tube that stretches the entire length of the property. The tube intersects a phthalo-green plinth clad in solid cement board panels with aluminum expansion channels. Each end of the tube is capped with aluminum fascia and a custom deck screen. Asked about cost, Killen says the most expensive item was the screen, which needed to be custom fabricated.

To enter the condo unit, one climbs a narrow stair to be greeted by a long corridor brightly lit by opaque south-facing windows. Killen didn't like the rooftop views of the adjacent commercial buildings. In the center of the main stairwell is a large, rectilinear casework piece that cantilevers playfully into the space allowing cutouts and

counters for books and objets d'art. Climbing the stairs from the second-floor entry hall puts one in the main living space, an open-plan layout. Killen is not shy about built-ins. The fireplace surround is a large piece of casework canted at a 30-degree angle from the wall and framing a huge flat-screen TV. Adjacent to the fireplace is a cantilevered bench that sits comfortably under a window with a partial view of the beach and ocean. The condo unit's two levels provide more than enough room for a small family and a few extra rooms for the owner's design studio. Logically, most of the unit faces west with ocean views while the first-floor office faces the east and the last public street before the beach.

In a sea of eclectic buildings, derelict structures and trendy cafes, 139 Hermosa Avenue makes a definitive and welcome statement of modernity, regionalism, and humor that symbolizes the Southern California lifestyle.

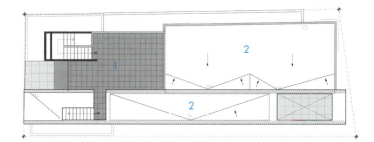

Roof plan
1. Roof deck
2. Built-up roof with white gravel sloping toward drain

Third floor plan
1. Deck
2. Bedroom 4
3. Closet
4. Bathroom 3
5. Walk-in closet
6. Powder room
7. Bedroom 3
8. Dining
9. Kitchen
10. Living

Second floor plan
1. Mechanical
2. Commercial space
3. Laundry
4. Bedroom 2
5. Bathroom 2
6. Walk-in closet
7. Master bedroom
8. Master bathroom

First floor plan
1. Residential entry
2. Restroom
3. Commercial space
4. Commercial parking
5. Residential garage

Working with a "Postage Stamp" Lot

Dean Nota Architect

Dean Nota looks like an architect. His face is framed by a shock of gray hair and a well-trimmed goatee. His keen brown eyes reveal the quiet but well-educated demeanor of an artist. Nota is one of those people who always wanted to be an architect. He was in the founding class at SCI-Arc, the legendary school of architecture in Santa Monica, and has remained close to its founders and the school. He worked for Ray Kappe for a number of years and served as a member of SCI-Arc's faculty.

Nota doesn't look like a beach bum, but he has lived near the ocean for most of his life. His work has featured almost exclusively in the beach towns that dot the coastline south of Los Angeles. Because of their small lots and quirky citizenry, the towns are a riot of eclectic architectural design. Victorian re-creations sit beside faux-Italianate palaces, which loom over 1950s suburban ranchers. Within this mix Nota has found fertile ground for modern architectural expression. Starting in the mid 1980s, Nota designed modern beach houses that turned people's heads and provided the impetus for a small design revolution in Southern California beach towns. Working with a palate of simple forms, glass blocks, and steel-rail detailing, he created a style that has been widely imitated throughout the region.

House 413 is a typical Nota creation. It is a small house covering almost the entirety of its 10-by-15-meter site. The house fills the permissible building envelope leaving little room to spare.

Nota says that he loves working with difficult sites and this certainly is one. Manhattan Beach is subdivided into alleys and streets that are really pedestrian walkways. Vehicular access is limited to the alleys where House 413 sits on its half lot. With space at a premium, Nota opted to use the top story as one large open living space and the second story for the master bedroom suite. The first story was reserved for parking and a guest bedroom and bath. An open-frame steel staircase that runs up the left side of the building is illuminated by a large glass-block wall and an oversized skylight on top that cants at 10 degrees. The large skylight and wraparound clerestories on the top floor bathe the main living space in sunlight most of the day. The main bedroom is divided from the circulation corridor by translucent sliding glass panels that provide ample illumination while maintaining privacy. The canted bay is clad in 33-centimeter-wide stainless-steel shingles that add a bit of shine and reflectance to the otherwise neutral gray stucco exterior.

As with most of Nota's buildings, House 413 is designed from the inside out. The only visible exterior façade faces a nondescript alley of mostly dull rear sides of compact beachside houses. A translucent glass entry and garage door and a sparkling stainless steel-clad upper bay give the street some cheer. Nota's work is deceptively subtle in its simplicity. House 413 is no exception. It makes a quiet yet definitive statement in a very eclectic architectural environment.

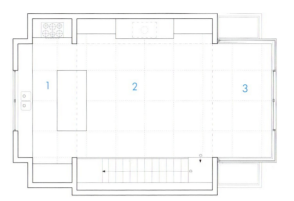

Third floor plan
1 Kitchen
2 Living
3 Dining

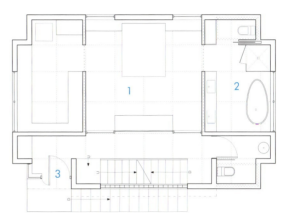

Second floor plan
1 Master bedroom
2 Master ensuite
3 Entrance

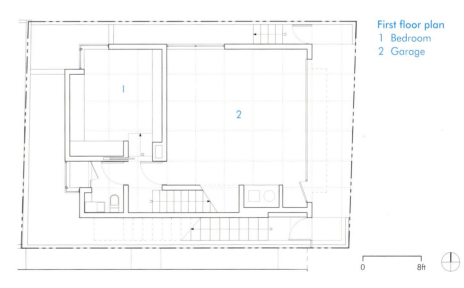

First floor plan
1 Bedroom
2 Garage

Upbeat Modern in a Quirky Monterey Bay Town

Flesher + Foster Architects

The Monterey Peninsula is hardly that. Rather, it is a bulge of land that gracefully projects into the Pacific Ocean at the southern end of Monterey Bay. It is neither San Francisco nor Los Angeles. It is Steinbeck country: home to moribund sardine canneries and emerald fields of artichokes and lettuce. Graced with a mild climate and a spectacular coastline, Monterey and its surrounding communities have been retreats and vacation spots for Californians for generations. Some of the world's most legendary golf courses—Pebble Beach, Spyglass, and Spanish Bay—are on the peninsula. The town of Carmel was home to Ansel Adams, Edward Westin, and other members of fine art photography's Group f/64 School of the 1930s and 1940s. It is here, among the cypresses and pines that architect William Foster chose to hang his hat and practice his modern style.

Bill Foster grew up in California's Central Valley, a vast agricultural region known worldwide for its production of fruits and vegetables. Designing buildings is something that fascinated him from a young age. When he was eight, a relative gave him a miniature drafting set so he could put his creations on paper. At U.C. Berkeley, he was influenced by the work of the popular regional architectural luminaries, Charles Moore, Joseph Esherick, and William Turnbull. In the early 1980s, he felt the need to change his living situation and move to either a big city, New York, or a small coastal community, Monterey. He chose Monterey. The small-town charm and exceptional beauty of the central coast kept him there.

Being a modernist in an intrinsically socially conservative environment is always an uphill battle. The Monterey Peninsula is a bit like the north shore of Long Island or some of the communities of Cape Cod; a place to play and build your vacation home. People don't acquire wealth in Monterey; they come there to spend the money they have already made.

Resort towns certainly have their attractions: the weather, the ocean, the view, and the solitude. The Monterey Peninsula has all that and it has provided Foster with a steady stream of clients who didn't want the cookie cutter Spanish Revival home so common in most California communities. When Jim Hebert and Ronnie Sarmanian came to Foster, they were looking for that solitude as a respite from their pressure-cooker corporate lifestyles at a major computer software firm. They owned a small, ramshackle house on a very small lot with a breathtaking view of Monterey Bay in the town of Pacific Grove.

Pacific Grove was once a religious encampment and the lots were divided as tent lots for religious revivals. When the religious fervor of the 19th century faded, people bought the lots and built very small homes. Although the geography varies, Pacific Grove has the architectural character of Hermosa or Redondo Beach: an almost madcap conglomeration of architectural styles and pretences.

Tearing down a 300-square-meter cottage and building a new 850-square-meter house on roughly the same footprint can be a daunting task, especially on a lot facing the ocean. Foster says

there was strong opposition to tearing down the existing cottage, but, ironically, almost none to its replacement. Foster's solution was a compact two-story structure whose main living spaces were on the second floor with bedrooms and parking on the first. Wraparound ocean views were afforded to the living and dining spaces while more pedestrian rooms (kitchen, bathroom, laundry) were relegated to the rear of the building. A small, but cozy patio garden with outdoor fireplace and privacy wall was placed on the alley side of the building, providing a sheltered outdoor living space. This compact house makes a definitive and uplifting statement on a street filled with eccentric and eclectic oceanfront homes. It neither fights with nor blends in to the shoreline's residential scale. Foster's Hebert residence is empirical proof that modernism can exist happily in a small-scale residential environment.

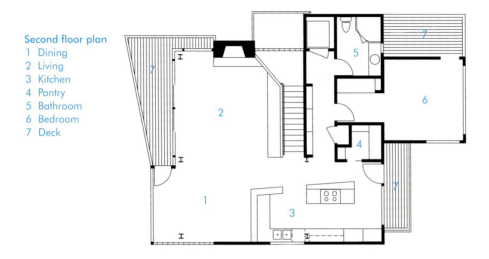

Second floor plan
1. Dining
2. Living
3. Kitchen
4. Pantry
5. Bathroom
6. Bedroom
7. Deck

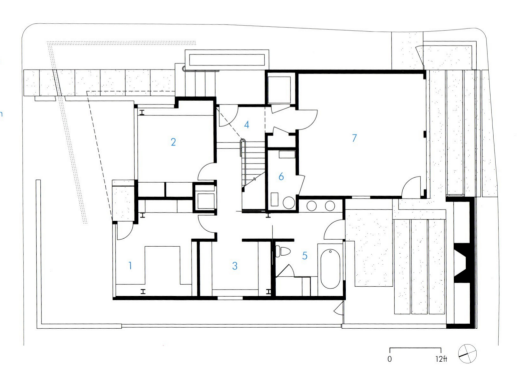

First floor plan
1. Master bedroom
2. Bedroom
3. Closet
4. Entry
5. Master bathroom
6. Mechanical
7. Garage

205

COUNTRY HOUSES

4

A Master's Touch in Carmel Valley

Jerrold E Lomax, FAIA: Architect

Jerrold Lomax is one of the unsung heroes of modern architecture in Southern California. He was one of the early innovators of modernism in the 1960s and has continued to practice for more than 60 years. Architects that know him speak of him in the most venerable of terms. He was the lead architect in Craig Ellwood's office in the 1950s, where he worked on two groundbreaking Case Study Houses. With his own office established in 1962, he has gone on to complete more than 200 buildings in both Northern and Southern California. In 1976 he was included in the *Los Angeles 12* exhibit put together by the Pacific Design Center and California Polytechnic University at Pomona. Among the other participants were the leading architects of Southern California: Cesar Pelli, Frank Gehry, and Ray Kappe. At 83, Lomax is a vibrant, creative man, living in a small town on Monterey Bay and still practicing.

Lomax started life in Southern California, but his family moved to Houston, Texas when he was 11. He joined the navy towards the end of the Second World War and was stationed in Japan where he developed an appreciation for Japanese architecture and design. At the end of his tour of duty, he enrolled at the School of Architecture at the University of Houston. Upon graduation, and after working in Houston for two years, Lomax returned to Southern California in 1953. Lomax had seen the work of Craig Ellwood in magazines and sought him out upon his return. Ellwood was a charismatic and articulate architect with a strong reputation, who happened to need an associate. Lomax turned out to be that person. Ellwood shared his great ideas and Lomax quickly began to contribute his own ideas. Together they collaborated on a number of award-winning projects in the Los Angeles area.

Nine years later, Lomax established his own firm in Venice, California, designing residences, commercial, and industrial buildings. In 1995 he sold his office to his then partner and moved to the Monterey Peninsula to start the next phase in his architectural career. He and his wife purchased a hillside lot in the scenic Carmel Valley just east of the city of Monterey in 1996 to build their award-winning residence and office. At the same time, he began designing the Ashton-Cassella residence, which is juxtaposed on the same knoll overlooking the bucolic valley below. As with much of Lomax's work, the complexity is hidden behind a simple cube of concrete block and glass. The house has floor-to-ceiling window walls at each end and a significant skylight running down the middle of the main living space, providing both views and ample illumination. Sharon Cassella-Ashton, sharing Lomax's love of Japanese design, filled the home with Japanese motifs, while interior designer Jorie Clark also responded with the selection of interior furnishings. A Japanese *koi* pond, filled with fish, sits in the middle of the main room and runs half its length. Off the main living space is an *ofuro*, a Japanese-style bath, built on grade and set next to a bamboo-lined private garden. The front yard is a *karesansui*, a raked gravel Zen garden, complete with Shinto monoliths. The rear patio on the west side of the house is covered with a deep overhang, which provides shade and limits heat gain from the western sunlight. Without green tiled and gabled roofs or *shoji* screens, the Ashton-Cassella house represents a modernist Japanese pavilion in the picturesque Carmel Valley of Central California.

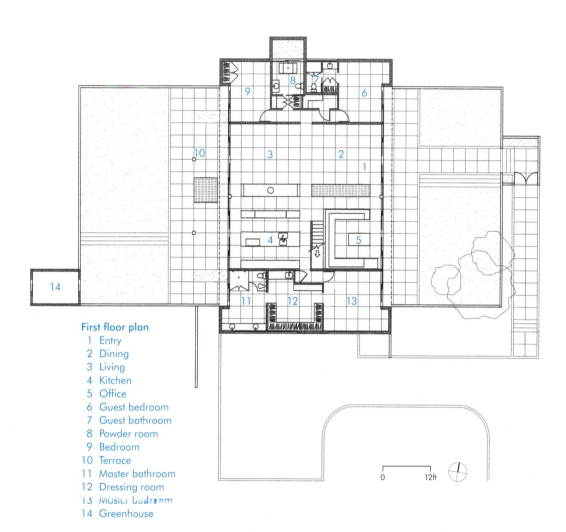

First floor plan
1. Entry
2. Dining
3. Living
4. Kitchen
5. Office
6. Guest bedroom
7. Guest bathroom
8. Powder room
9. Bedroom
10. Terrace
11. Master bathroom
12. Dressing room
13. Master bedroom
14. Greenhouse

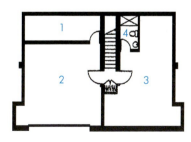

Basement plan
1. Storage
2. Garage
3. Workshop
4. Bathroom

Getting Down to Basics

Jim Jennings Architecture

One can think of Jim Jennings as the architect's architect. His office is small and its volume is modest, but each of his projects garners the attention of the architectural press both nationally and internationally. His buildings, deceptively simple in design but often iconic in nature, make statements that reverberate far beyond the San Francisco Bay Area. His work, characterized by simple geometric forms and clean lines, has an almost sculptural quality to it, reminiscent of a Joseph Albers' painting, three colored squares carefully nested into each other and nothing more.

A native of Southern California, Jennings migrated north to study engineering at Berkeley in the 1960s. While crossing campus one day he came across a critique session of an architecture class being held in an outdoor courtyard. He sat in and was entranced. The next semester, he transferred out of engineering and into architecture and has been there ever since. After earning his degree he got a job working with Ezra Ehrenkrantz studying a systems approach to housing for U.C. Berkeley. After Ehrenkrantz he migrated over to SOM's Washington, D.C. office where he worked on large-scale urban planning projects. He opened his office in San Francisco in 1976, a time of economic upheaval in the United States. His early work was mostly individual homes, although he also did hospital and commercial remodels. His first significant commission was the remodel of World Savings corporate offices, which won several awards.

The Visiting Artists' House was initially designed in the early 1990s, but not built until more than a decade later. The house is situated on a large ranch located about 100 kilometers north of San Francisco. The ranch is owned by a successful Bay Area builder and arts patron who runs the ranch as an art preserve. Noted sculptors from around the world are invited to stay at the ranch and execute large-scale projects on the 64-hectare site. As part of the ranch's program, the artists are required to live on the site for a few weeks to formulate their proposals and experience the ambiance of the bucolic environs. Once their projects are accepted, they return to the ranch to complete and install them on the property.

The house is a half-below-grade slice into a slight hill supported by two 30-centimeter-thick concrete walls that run its length and are almost parallel. The walls delineate both the house and its exterior spaces and are its entire structure. The house is laid out as two almost-identical suites that mirror each other. The central courtyard is shared by two living rooms providing a space for dialog between two artists staying at the same time. The house is minimalist in almost every detail with the exception of the concrete walls that have a carved, geometric, bas-relief pattern, the work of noted sculptor David Rabinowitch of New York. Skylights run along the edge of the concrete walls illuminating the bas-relief patterns at different times of the day. In some ways, the house becomes a life-sized piece of sculpture that alternately provides shelter for the artists. The Visiting Artists' House represents something of a clean slate allowing ample room for creative types to exercise their imaginations in a pristine environment.

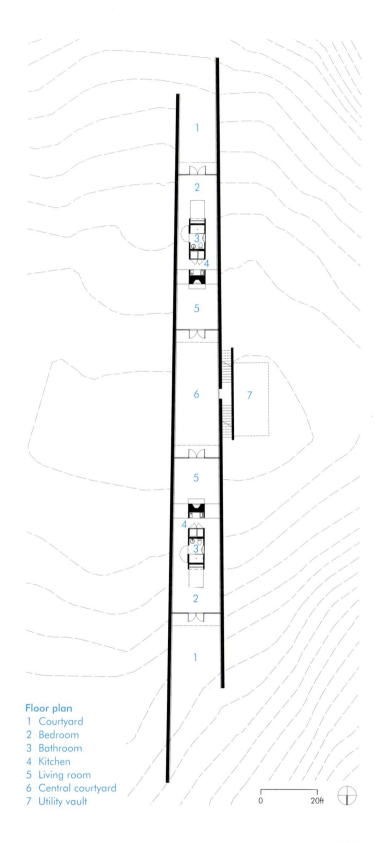

Floor plan
1. Courtyard
2. Bedroom
3. Bathroom
4. Kitchen
5. Living room
6. Central courtyard
7. Utility vault

Desert Living, Prefabricated

Marmol Radziner

As is true with so many Californians, Leo Marmol, FAIA, and Ron Radziner, FAIA, are both first-generation Americans. Marmol's parents emigrated from Cuba to Los Angeles via northern California in the 1950s. Radziner's family survived the Holocaust in Europe and immigrated to Los Angeles in the 1950s also. Radziner says that his family inspired him "to live life and do something I loved. Building, making things, is all I ever wanted to do," he says.

Marmol and Radziner attended California Polytechnic State University in San Luis Obispo where they earned their degrees in architecture. They were friends at Cal Poly but several years passed before they decided to open their firm in Los Angeles in 1989. Four years later they were hired to carry out the restoration of Richard Neutra's Kaufmann house in Palm Springs. The house was one of Neutra's last works and was made famous by Julius Shuman's legendary photographs in 1947. Marmol Radziner has since been involved in the restoration of mid-20th-century modern houses by Cliff May, Rudolph Schindler, John Lautner, and Thornton Ladd. Needless to say, they developed an intimate knowledge of the work of mid-20th-century masters.

Marmol Radziner is a design/build firm actively involved in the construction of many of its projects. The architects see managing the construction as an important part of the creative process.

As an outgrowth of their involvement in construction, Marmol Radziner developed a modular home system based on a 3.65-by-16.7-by-4-meter unit that can be easily built, finished in a factory, and shipped to a site via any U.S. highway. The units are almost completely finished in the factory with siding, windows, doors, HVAC, and finishes in place. At the site, they are placed on prebuilt foundations and fastened together. While comparable in price to standard "stick built" houses, the modular house offers the advantages of quality control, rapid delivery times, and a multitude of eco-friendly components.

Marmol Radziner's prototype modular house is the Desert House, built in Desert Hot Springs, about 170 kilometers east of Los Angeles. The house sits on a slight rise on an expansive 20,000-square-meter site with dramatic desert views. It is fabricated from four modular interior units and six deck units that provide covered outdoor living spaces. Almost half the enclosed area of the house is covered decking. The main living areas of the house have wraparound fenestration, but are shielded from the unforgiving midday desert sun by deep overhangs and enclosed deck areas. The house has an L-shaped configuration with one area comprising the main structure and the other the guest quarters and a small painting studio. A pool and a fire pit are framed by the L-shaped configuration. Solar panels on the roof of the main building provide most of the house's electricity. The concrete floors, white sheet-rock walls, and simple modern furnishings become an unobtrusive backdrop to the ever-changing desert landscape. Marmol Radziner's in-house woodhop crafted most of the furniture items and all of the casework. Used primarily as a weekend home, the house opens up to the outdoor spaces seamlessly, creating an inviting environment for entertaining and relaxed desert living.

Floor plan
1. Bedroom
2. Kitchen
3. Mechanical
4. Bathroom
5. Great room
6. Covered deck
7. Patio
8. Studio
9. Pool

237

Wine Country Simplicity

Edmonds + Lee

Robert Edmonds says he doesn't like Maybeck. For Bay Area architects that is something of a blasphemy. Maybeck, an early 20th-century classicist turned modern, is a seminal figure to many architects. But for Edmonds, he is just an impediment. Instead he takes his cultural inspiration from European modernists and their mid-20th-century progeny. Edmonds grew up in the San Francisco Bay Area and studied architecture at California Polytechnic University, San Luis Obispo. Needing a change of scenery, Edmonds migrated east. He enrolled in the graduate program in architecture at Columbia University in New York City. While there, he met his wife and partner, Vivian Lee. After graduating they stayed in New York and found work with a variety of nationally known firms, from Steven Holl to Skidmore, Owings & Merrill, where they worked on a variety of high-end residential and museum projects. New York can be an exciting place to live and work if you are a young architect, but it can also be very limiting. Edmonds and Lee eventually decided to make their way westward to San Francisco in 2005 and together they established Edmonds + Lee Architects.

In 2007 they landed a commission to design the Summerhill house in Sonoma County, part of California's historic wine-producing region. Sonoma Valley, lined on each side by 1000-meter-high mountains, is one of California's more picturesque valleys.

Summerhill house is on 16 hectares and flanked by pastureland, vineyards, and orchards. The house was designed to be a weekend retreat for a young executive based about an hour away in San Francisco. The house sits on a rise in the center of the property and is segmented into three separate structures arranged around a large lawn and swimming pool. The buildings are simple cedar-clad rectangles with triangular sliced fenestration that wraps around each end. Edmonds oriented the main house to fully capture the mountain views, the textures and colors of which change throughout the day. The triangular windows become an inverse metaphor for the surrounding hills. The main living space is a large volume bisected by a metal-screened flue. It is bright, cheery, and well proportioned. The finishes are white, simple, and unadorned allowing the dramatic views to stand out as the primary decoration. The main and guest houses are surrounded by wide decking that is elevated half a meter from grade and doubles as a bench. The minimalist landscaping sharpens rather than softens the edges of the buildings as they silhouette against the verdant hillsides.

Simple in its plan and powerful in its execution, Edmonds + Lee have created a new California single-family icon in one of its most bucolic and beautiful places.

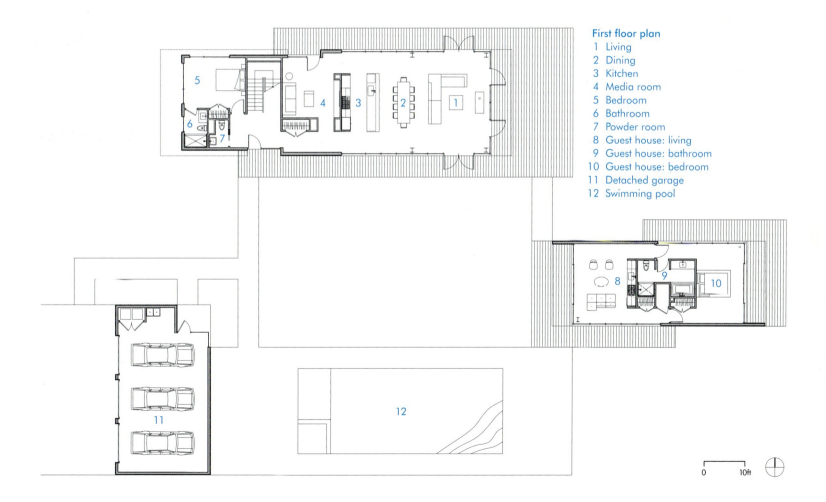

249

Acknowledgments

This book represents the culmination of many years of work photographing and befriending hundreds of architects in California. Two architects, one in Northern California and one in Southern California, have been particularly helpful in guiding me in my selection process. Robert Swatt in the Bay Area has been asking me to create this book for some time and has been very supportive. Stephen Kanner in Los Angeles has gone out of his way to give me guidance and introduce me to Southern California's vibrant design community. I would also like to thank Jorie Clark of Carmel Valley who was the interior designer on several of these projects. Many years ago, she was the first person to make me aware of the Case Study House program and has been a strong supporter of modernism and my photography ever since. Finally, I wish to thank Alessina Brooks and Paul Latham, publishers of The Images Publishing Group, for giving me the opportunity to write and photograph this beautiful book. Without their support, *California Cool* would just be another good idea.

Index of Architects

Callas Shortridge architects   130
shortridgearchitects.com
callasarchitects.com

Cigolle X Coleman   12
cxcarch.com

David Hertz Architects Inc.,   146
Studio of Environmental Architecture
studioea.com

Dean Nota Architect   186
nota.net

Edmonds + Lee   238
edmondslee.com

Ehrlich Architects   158
s-ehrlich.com

Jerrold Lomax Architect   208
jelomax.com

Jim Jennings Architecture   218
jimjenningsarchitecture.com

Johnson Fain   102
johnsonfain.com

Kanner Architects   44
kannerarch.com

Macy Architecture   120
macyarchitecture.com

Marmol Radziner   226
marmol-radziner.com

Ray Kappe, F.A.I.A   84
rkappe@verizon.net

Regan Bice Architects   94
reganbice.com

Seidel Architects   172
seidelarchitects.com

Studio 9 one 2   178
studio9one2.com

Studio Pali Fekete architects [SPF:a]   58
spfa.com

Swatt Architects   68
swattmiers.com

WA design   28
wadesign.com

William E. Foster Architecture   194
wmefoster@att.net

Every effort has been made to trace the original source of copyright material contained in this book. The publishers would be pleased to hear from copyright holders to rectify any errors or omissions.

The information and illustrations in this publication have been prepared and supplied by the author. While all reasonable efforts have been made to source the required information and ensure accuracy, the publishers do not, under any circumstances, accept responsibility for errors, omissions, and representations express or implied.